ITIL® Small-scale Implementation

Sharon Taylor

Ivor Macfarlane

 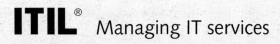

London: TSO

Published by TSO (The Stationery Office) and available from:

Online
www.tsoshop.co.uk

Mail, Telephone, Fax & E-mail
TSO
PO Box 29, Norwich, NR3 1GN
Telephone orders/General enquiries: 0870 6005522
Fax orders: 0870 6005533
E-mail: customer.services@tso.co.uk
Textphone 0870 240 3701

TSO Shops
123 Kingsway, London WC2B 6PQ
020 7242 6393 Fax 020 7242 6394
68–69 Bull Street, Birmingham B4 6AD
0121 236 9696 Fax 0121 236 9699
9–21 Princess Street, Manchester M60 8AS
0161 834 7201 Fax 0161 833 0634
16 Arthur Street, Belfast BT1 4GD
028 9023 8451 Fax 028 9023 5401
18–19 High Street, Cardiff CF10 1PT
029 2039 5548 Fax 029 2038 4347
71 Lothian Road, Edinburgh EH3 9AZ
0870 606 5566 Fax 0870 606 5588

TSO Accredited Agents
(see Yellow Pages)

and through good booksellers

For further information on OGC products, contact:

OGC Service Desk
Rosebery Court
St Andrews Business Park
Norwich NR7 0HS

Telephone +44 (0) 845 000 4999

First published 2005

Second impression 2006

ISBN 0 11 330980 5

Printed in the United Kingdom for The Stationery Office

CONTENTS

FOREWORD

There has been much popular demand for this book and we are pleased to see that the OGC is now making it available in an updated form. The original version of this book, entitled *ITIL Practices in Small IT Units*, was published in 1995 as part of the first series of ITIL best practice guidance books and was very well received.

Since then, the IT Infrastructure Library has undergone numerous changes and many members of the ITSM community have asked for an updated version of the original book. This updated version is now available and is the final publication in the current version of ITIL.

The international *it*SMF organisation, through its International Publications Executive Sub-Committee (IPESC), comprising members from all *it*SMF chapters around the world, has given formal *it*SMF International endorsement to this book.

The IPESC is proud to be the official endorsement body for OGC ITSM publications. The review process is a rigorous one, with stringent criteria that any ITSM-related publication must satisfy before it can be endorsed. IPESC endorsement of this book demonstrates a solid partnership between the OGC and the *it*SMF community, and the OGC's commitment to continue to produce high quality and valuable ITIL publications.

Through the efforts and dedication of its committee members, the IPESC aims to create added value for the community of ITSM professionals by enabling the development of a common global library that supports a uniform standard of ITSM knowledge and best practices.

On behalf of the *it*SMF global community, I wish to thank the OGC for providing this book and the IPESC for their dedication, effort and commitment in reviewing and endorsing it.

I know you will find the book enjoyable, informative and useful in your pursuit of IT Service Management excellence.

Sharon Taylor
Chair, International Publications Executive Sub-Committee
*it*SMF International

ACKNOWLEDGEMENTS

Authors

Sharon Taylor, Aspect Group Inc
Ivor Macfarlane, Guillemot Rock

This book is a revision of the earlier ITIL book, and so it is appropriate to recognise significant contributions to that original product made by Jenny Ellwood-Wade and Tony Jenkins.

The authors would also like to thank those who gave their time to review this book:
J. Andrew Atencio, City of Greenwood Village, Colorado, US
Janaki Chakravarthy, Infosys Technologies Limited, India
Alison Cartlidge, Xansa, UK
Karen Ferris, ProActive Services, Australia
Chris Jones, Ariston Strategic Consulting, Australia
Christian F. Nissen, Itilligence, Denmark
Doug Read, Pro-Attivo, UK
Sue Shaw, Tricentrica, UK
Jan van Bon, *it*SMF Netherlands

Thanks also to:
Janine Eves of TSO and Chris Lang of *it*SMF UK for project management, constructive cajoling and support in getting the book delivered and published.

1 INTRODUCTION

1.1 Background

In 1995, the UK Government's Central Computer and Telecommunications Agency (CCTA), now subsumed within the Office of Government Commerce (OGC), published a book entitled *ITIL Practices in Small IT Units*. Following the completion of the declared range of ITIL books, this was the first so-called complementary book, intended to help those adopting the ITIL guidance within small organisations.

At that time, the best-known and publicised ITIL implementations in the IT Service Management (ITSM) community were in large organisations. Smaller organisations who set out to implement ITIL found that a degree of scaled adaptation was needed to make the most use of ITIL best practices. The 1995 book was published to provide guidance to smaller IT organisations in scaling the concepts and to help them in their pursuit of service excellence using the ITIL best practices.

ITIL was revamped in 2000–2002 and the second version was process focused rather than function oriented. The revised version of ITIL was conceived to be inherently scaleable and, indeed, since then, many hundreds of organisations, from very small through to the largest multinationals, have adopted and adapted ITIL guidance.

The purpose of this book is to reacquaint IT organisations both large and small with how the implementation of ITIL best practices can be scaled to meet the constraints facing almost any IT organisation today.

The book is based upon a simple truth: ITIL works for every size and type of company. The scalability of implementation is the key to success. Within this book we offer some explanation of why and how smaller organisations are different, and offer some ideas and techniques that might help smaller ITSM organisations to improve the quality of the service they deliver to their customers and users.

Although the older book has been extensively revisited and updated, nothing has been altered for the sake of change alone – the 1995 book sold and was used extensively, and we hope that we have retained the strengths of that book which made it useful, while adding some new ideas of relevance to the twenty-first century.

1.2 Scope

This is not a book about ITIL shortcuts or cutting corners – it is not about Service Management as a finite set of things that can be done, and choosing which ones not to do.

Successful Service Management, the kind that supports the business customers and delivers business services, relies on a broad understanding and implementation of the Service Management processes. This book considers how the circumstances of delivering effective IT Service Management are affected by the situations and constraints that typically occur within a small organisation, and how to get good results quickly by adapting the ITIL advice to circumstance.

1.2.1 Where this guide fits into ITIL

The ITIL books can be seen as providing a bridge between the technology and the business and, like all bridges, to be useful this one must span the whole gap. A free booklet is available from the IT Service Management Forum (*it*SMF) setting out the coverage of these books. See www.itsmf.com

The scope of this book covers all elements of ITIL making up that bridge. At its centre lies the accepted 'core' of ITIL – the Service Support and Service Delivery processes – and there will be a degree of concentration there. However, context and communication are vital, especially in a small organisation, and IT Service Management must interface with neighbouring processes.

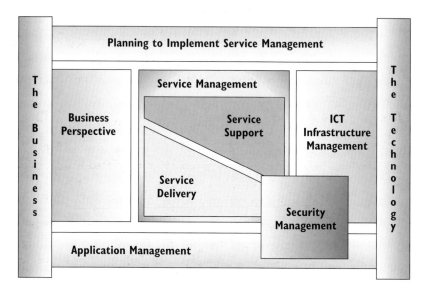

Figure 1.1 Structure of the ITIL guidance

1.2.2 The focus of this text

The mainstream ITIL books were written with larger IT organisations in mind, around a concept of time and resource availability to drive improvements. Clearly this is not the only environment in which IT service improvements are needed. Indeed many, if not most, organisations will have constrained circumstances to work within, including:

- small budgets and staff numbers
- disproportionate IT support organisations
- minimal disposable budgets to investigate new initiatives
- restricted time frames in which to demonstrate improvement
- restricted collaboration from colleagues and customers
- a stable organisation with significant resistance to innovation.

This book will focus on the constraints and the opportunities that accompany improving ITSM in a small organisation. However, many of the ideas explored and suggestions delivered will be relevant and useful to any organisation struggling with constraints. In practice, it is unlikely that any organisation will be subject to only one such constraint.

The book can also be of use to organisations with restrictions on headcount, seeking to achieve economies and advice on the combination of roles.

1.3   ITIL in context

ITIL does not stand alone but fits into an ITSM best practice context. And, of course, small organisations will have need of best practice in areas such as project management, risk management etc. which will impact upon Service Management.

1.3.1   Formal standard in IT Service Management

A formal standard for IT Service Management was published by the British Standards Institution as BS15000; this has been republished by other national standards bodies in Australia, South Africa, Hungary and Korea. In 2005 this was accepted by the international standards organisation (ISO) to be ISO20000.

The first organisations to achieve BS15000 certification were small IT organisations, which demonstrated its applicability to small organisations. Small organisations can reap much the same benefits as larger ones, including demonstration that the IT organisation:

- follows accepted good practice
- satisfies external (and maybe also internal) customer demands for conformance
- acts as a focal point and target for service improvement.

Practice has shown that smaller organisations can achieve certification to this standard faster and more easily than larger ones. Reasons for this include:

- shorter lines of communication make demonstration of conformant practices easier

- service improvement requirements can be demonstrated in a shorter time frame
- smaller, more reactive organisations seem better able to mobilise resources and encourage the commitment required.

1.4 The significance of size

How small is *small*? However big or small an organisation is, delivering benefits with constrained resources is bound to be relevant, and therefore many of the ideas and principles addressed in this book will have wide relevance. We focus here on two specific target groups:

- organisations delivering IT services with limited fiscal resource
- IT organisations with a low ratio of IT staff to customers.[1]

What is significant in both these situations is that compromises are required in the form of amalgamation of roles, simplification of processes, reduced resilience etc. It is certain that any application of the ITIL guidance will require adaptation because:

- There are a lot of small organisations and, as the importance of ITSM is recognised across all sectors, small organisations realise that it makes sense for them to adopt the ITIL guidance
- ITIL has (wrongly) been accused of being overly bureaucratic and requiring large numbers of managers and specialists to deliver. This inevitably puts off small organisations, where there simply is not the resource to separate roles and tasks. In fact, combination of roles can increase the effectiveness of ITIL
- Smaller organisations tend to be less formal than larger ones, and this informality often manifests itself in a casual approach to using structured processes
- Smaller organisations have less specialism, to the extent that ITSM is only one part of the group's responsibility
- Managers (and their staff) working in small organisations are inevitably working closer to the front line, have less time and money to investigate improvement initiatives and approaches, and, crucially, may well dismiss the ITIL approach as too complex and resource-hungry to be appropriate to them.

Here, we will demonstrate that the ITIL guidance has a significant role to play for all organisations, large and small.

---

1 This refers to small IT organisations supporting small business organisations – it does not refer to the kind of small IT organisation that supports a large business structure, typically through the use of significant outsourced staff resource.

1.5 Understanding the term 'small'

Already, we have used the term 'small' in relation to an IT organisation. Intuitively this makes sense but it is not easy to find meaningful ways strictly to define an IT organisation as being small. However, we do need to understand in general terms what we mean by the term so that we may set out the kinds of organisations that will find this book most relevant and useful.

Size can often be a relative measure. For example, some large companies have IT organisations which are small in relation to their overall size. Conversely, small companies may have large IT organisations.

Size is often related to the complexity of the IT environment itself and the need for a proportionately sized IT organisation to manage it. It is neither possible nor overly useful to make any particular assumptions about the technology that small IT organisations support – many will be innovative technologically; others may be supporting established legacy systems on ageing technologies. Indeed it is common for small organisations to combine supporting older services in tandem with some degree of innovation. What we are concerned with in this book are the processes that they use to manage the services and to deliver effective support to the business processes of which they form a part.

Size can also just be an absolute measure, as in the example of a small company with a small IT organisation.

In either case, these IT organisations will have similar constraints that make scaleable ITIL processes the recommended approach.

While every IT organisation is unique, there are certain characteristics that are inherent in small ones.

1.6 Characteristics of small organisations

If you think of any organisation as a community of people, you see that each has distinct nuances and interactions. If you then change the magnitude of the community, you see those nuances and interactions change dramatically. No matter where on earth you look, this is true. There are significant differences in the characteristics of small and large organisations.

Let's consider the size of IT organisations from a village and city perspective, and the differences between them. These differences can be summarised by comparing the small IT organisation to a village and the larger organisation to a city (see Figure 1.2). The most important indication from this analogy is not about size or any actual characteristics of human villages or cities – it is that the important differences are based on attitudes and behaviour, and upon the familiarity with the circumstances, opportunities and constraints that come from the immediate environment we live or work in. The relative merits of village and city life have been long debated elsewhere.[2] The important point is that there are fundamental differences which have to be recognised and accounted for. Different kinds of approaches and solutions are required in each case.

Village	City
Informal culture	Formal culture
Team spirit	Competitiveness
Quick communication	Slow communication
Responsive	Tendency to inertia
Flexible	Constrained
Understanding of the business	Isolation from the business
Relying on individuals	Broad pool of expertise
Nowhere to hide	Role flexibility
Wide knowledge	Specialisms
Limited knowledge	Comprehensive knowledge
High organisation costs	Economies of scale
Per capita complexity	Role division

Figure 1.2 Village-city comparison

1.6.1 Informal culture

One way of addressing the differences is to compare the interactions amongst the staff (through which much of the process is delivered) to those that take place in society. Then, whatever the technology or even the number of staff, small organisations can be expected to share common characteristics which differentiate them from larger ones.

Perhaps the most obvious and immediately noticeable difference between small and large IT organisations is organisational culture. The small group is a close environment where everyone knows – or thinks they know – everyone else's business. Within a small IT organisation, there is often a relatively informal atmosphere, as people know each other and are aware of their abilities, likely reactions, attitudes, prejudices and perspectives etc.

---

2 Potter (1918).

This contrasts with the environments of larger IT organisations, where procedures and formality are much more prevalent, and submissions and requests are more impersonal, aimed at fitting rules rather than people's views. (That said, understanding the decision-makers' reactions and wishes is a major asset in seeking approval for changes and innovation in any size of organisation.)

However, informality is not always a good thing. It can result in serious risks, especially where disciplines such as Configuration Management or Change Management are concerned. Some degree of formality is a necessary part of managing; without it, small IT organisations can lose control over essential aspects of the service, with very costly results.

1.6.2 Team spirit

In a small organisation (whether it be an IT organisation, a sports team or any other group combining to deliver a common purpose) members are likely to see themselves as members of a single team, with common goals.

This sense of unity fades as the organisation grows in size. Here the environment is large enough to allow a number of internal teams to develop, with potential rivalry between the different IT branches. This can quickly block collaboration, whereas in small organisations the team sense is likely to expand beyond the walls of traditional ITSM and enable closer collaboration with testing, application development, procurement and other associated processes.

Illustration

Observers of sports (both professional and amateur) will have seen many more internal disagreements within football teams over the years than arguments between doubles pairs in tennis.

1.6.3 Quick communication

Good communication in a small organisation is almost inevitable since each person will be responsible for several roles. When there is a communication of interest, it will spread across the entire organisation quickly – often driven by gossip and social traffic.

This can encourage strong informal communications between the IT organisation and the business. These links help to ensure that things are done with the minimum number of complications, but can also lead to things happening without sufficient consideration, consultation and documentation, or even on occasion without financial or management approval.

In larger organisations, on the other hand, communication is almost always a problem. Everything must be formally recorded and procedures are needed to make sure all the right people are kept in touch with each other.

1.6.4 Responsive

Small IT organisations can be very responsive, developing and amending plans and procedures as they go. The sheer inertia that goes with large staff numbers is mostly absent, allowing for fast decisions in an environment small enough to canvass everybody's views within a day. This has the benefits of:

- *Allowing initiatives to get started with less planning* – this will be interpreted by the customer as a more caring and responsive IT service, so long as the initiatives are useful to the customer
- *Tailoring ideas during a project or service* – changes are easier because the decision-makers are more likely to be available and because the staff involved are much more likely to know the requirements and abilities of the rest of the IT organisation. Thus changes are more likely to be:
  - made quickly, for example, within a day
  - accepted by other staff
  - tailored to the customers' needs
- *Tailoring services to small numbers of staff* – providing a service to 5,000 users inevitably means that the users see it as centrally organised and imposed. The small IT organisation working within a small company has more chance to personalise its services. This can be especially valuable when there is a diverse range of users and customers, for example, R&D groups.

1.6.5 Flexible

Small organisations can react to changes and new ideas very quickly. 'Wheeler-dealing' is easier as a smaller number of staff means there are plenty of shortcuts available.

If something needs to be discussed or decided, all the major players can probably be brought together in the same room at the same time. New ideas are more likely to at least get attention, and probably get support.

Also, small organisations can dare to do things which larger organisations cannot because they can reach decision-makers and because, since everyone knows each other, less preliminary work is required in preparing and justifying initiatives.

1.6.6 Understanding of the business

The smaller an organisation, the more likely it is that those working within it can clearly see the supply and process chain that delivers the organisation's business products or services. This extends to the ITSM staff who, aware of their role in the overall organisation, have an advantage in tailoring their work to better fit the business needs.

1.6.7 Relying on individuals

Within small organisations, the reliance on one person to know things and be the local expert is inevitable. Only where there is a major risk to business viability can the cost of training extra people be justified.

It is probably wise to accept that there will be such heroes, but to take steps to make the best of the situation:

- try to plan properly for times they will be absent from the office
- document their existence, identify risks and frequently confirm they remain acceptable
- ensure they stay up to date in their field of expertise, attending relevant training events and conferences
- do what you can to retain them in the organisation through incentives and job satisfaction.

Small organisations have to be aware that staff can leave suddenly for a variety of unavoidable reasons, and make sure that functions can survive the departure of any one individual. So, while formal communication between separate sections is not usually necessary, it is vital to record what has been decided and what has been done.

1.6.8 Nowhere to hide

A small environment means that if things go wrong, there are fewer options for solving problems. For example, when there are personality clashes, there is little that can be done to prevent them from causing damage.

On the other hand, if there are personality clashes in larger organisations, staff can be moved around to minimise disruption and conflict. Larger organisations also have the ability to organise people into meaningful groups or sections, allowing them to become more expert in a particular aspect of IT.

1.6.9 Wide knowledge

Another problem that small IT organisations face is a lack of specialists.

Small organisations require specialists to deliver key functions. The specialists should know about customers' business practices and the latest developments in relevant areas. However, the inevitable restrictions upon the range of specialists and knowledge the small organisation can support means that any specialists must be carefully tuned to the organisation's needs.

Within a larger organisation, in contrast, there is more scope for people to concentrate exclusively on one specific area, working in relative isolation from the rest of the organisation and the business. This may have implications for training staff, especially when they face moving from a large IT organisation into a smaller one, something occurring more frequently as large organisations fragment under the pressures of outsourcing, downsizing and user empowerment.

The typical reality in a small IT organisation is a group with wide knowledge that encourages those who can to turn their hands to anything, or at least that favours those who can pick up new skills or apply familiar concepts to new areas. Most staff have to carry out different roles and are in regular contact with the business. This affects the way an organisation is structured, including grading and career paths, and the types of people who feel most comfortable in it.

All IT organisations have staff who specialise in keeping the infrastructure intact and service providers who use that infrastructure to provide the agreed levels of service. But a small organisation cannot afford many other specialists; the proportions of specialists in particular areas may be the same as for larger organisations, but absolute numbers are smaller. Vitally, small organisations are rarely in a position to have more than one specialist in any given subject area. Thus, both to provide a range of specialist services and to provide cover during staff absences, they are likely to need external suppliers or cross-service arrangements, finding a balance between the need for the specialism and how long it will be needed for.

Even in very small IT organisations, there can be particular specialisms that are best dealt with in-house. As business needs and the technical infrastructure evolve, the skills which are needed will also evolve. IT managers must be ready to acquire new skills as they think appropriate, and discard recognition and use of old skills. This may mean retraining or even releasing staff with knowledge that is no longer relevant to the way the organisation works.

1.6.10 Limited knowledge

Related to its relative lack of specialisms, the small IT organisation is also likely to have gaps in its knowledge base, since a few people cannot know everything.

To make the most of the skills that are available, small organisations often have to combine several roles (even potentially separate job functions) within a single post, using staff as generalists rather than specialists. Another way of maximising skills is to let the skills that are actually available define the structure of the organisation. This can be more efficient than trying to create a structure around a theoretical requirement. As staff change, the structure can be reorganised.

Where skills are not available in-house, small organisations can make use of specialist services from third-party suppliers, such as outside consultants, rather than trying to cope with their own limited resources. This reduces the specialist skills required within the organisation, and provides those skills economically for the short time they are needed. This is effectively a decision based on financial considerations. The topic is dealt with in detail in Section 4.10.

For the larger IT organisation, staff skills and specialisms are readily available, providing cover for absence and a second opinion on difficult questions.

1.6.11 High organisation costs

Small IT organisations are not in a position to benefit on their own from the economies of scale which may be available to larger organisations. This means that the total cost to the organisation of employing and supporting each member of IT staff will be higher, reflecting, among other things:

- higher training and skill levels – since specialisms are not sustainable, staff need to have knowledge of more areas and each will need a wider range of expertise
- higher relative costs of essential software tools
- cross-training can be more costly to a small organisation, but may well be critically important in protecting business services.

The cost of IT per user is also likely to be higher, not only for these reasons, but also because:

- hardware and software licence costs will be relatively higher
- relatively more consultancy will be required (although if funds for consultancy are not available this would result in lower service levels being delivered).

Generally, higher costs to operate small IT organisations add to the burden of constraints from an overall ITSM perspective.

1.6.12 Per capita complexity

It is a common misunderstanding that small means simple. In fact, many tasks are more complex on a modern small site, not less. Standard configurations are less likely with small diverse customer communities and a higher percentage of users are likely to use more fragile technologies, such as VPN (virtual private network) and e-mail to hand-helds. Compared to a larger organisation, for each customer (or ITSM staff member) there is likely to be a larger amount and more variety of:

- incidents
- Configuration Items and configuration relationships
- networking software and hardware
- applications, locations and usability issues.

Many small IT organisations, for example, those supporting scientific or research organisations, have a customer requirement that is highly complex and extremely dynamic.

On the other hand, some of the simplest IT organisations are very large, providing a few services to thousands of users. They have their own particular problems but, generally speaking, these are predictable ones. There is no obvious correlation between the difficulty of a job and the size of an IT organisation, despite claims from both large and small organisation staff that their tasks are inherently more difficult.

1.7 Deciding on the size of an IT organisation

Many organisations are faced with options concerning the size of their IT functions and also their ITSM sections. These options include:

- *A single ITSM function covering all sections of the organisation*
- *Multiple, small ITSM operations* – each is tailored to serve a particular part of the business and is located within an operational sub-organisation
- *Outsourcing all or part of the IT support service* – if organisations outsource, they need to consider what the optimum size for outsourced organisations should be. This is likely to be larger rather than smaller, moving towards economies of scale at the cost of a service tailored to the specific needs of the small organisation.

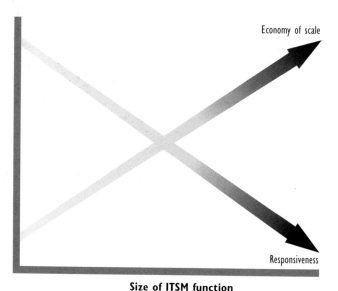

Economy of scale

Responsiveness

Size of ITSM function

Figure 1.3 Balance of service and per capita costs

In practice, the ideal situation for most organisations, whether in-house or outsourced, will lie somewhere between the two extremes of multiple, tiny IT set-ups and a single centralised function. In this way, a balance can be struck between the quality of a service tailored to users' needs and economies of scale (see Figure 1.3).

1.8   Scaling ITIL down for small IT organisations

Most managers want to take ideas which have proved valuable elsewhere and try them out in their own environment. This is sensible practice – it is after all the philosophy upon which ITIL is based. However, no two organisations are alike, and, in order to translate ideas successfully from one environment to another, processes and procedures must be adapted to fit.

While some ITIL processes scale down easily and function equally well in small or large environments, most will break if scaled down too far.

An underlying principle of this book is to consider how scaling down affects the functions in ITIL, and where possible to give ideas for adapting them. The questions to ask about scaling down are:

- is it still practicable?
- is it still desirable?
- do enough of the benefits remain?

If the answer to any of these questions is 'No', then it is time to find different ways of achieving the same result.

Scaling down processes to fit the workload expected and the resources available is the core of adapting generic best practices to small organisations. For example, in the smallest organisations, scaling down Incident Management processes may well deliver a requirement for less than one full-time person on the Service Desk. Simply declaring the Service Desk to be a part-time role or a task shared with others will not necessarily deliver the service as required. Techniques to approach this specific example are discussed in Section 4.4.2.

Properly managed, scaling down will bring the benefits of ITIL to small IT organisations.

Case example:
Supporting quality management – a question of scale

Consider an organisation which has introduced the principles of quality management and has accepted the figure of 3% of staff costs as an appropriate quality management overhead. With around 200 staff, this creates a quality management section of six staff, reporting directly to senior management and independent of the operational management structure (an ISO9000 requirement).

Convert this set-up to smaller establishments. With 100 staff, the quality section becomes three staff, and still functions. With fewer than 50 staff, however, there are problems. In a small organisation, 3% of staff costs might translate into one person. This means there is no depth of cover nor contingency for absence. It might also mean two or more people with a part-time role, inevitably compromising the independent reporting requirement.

Alternatives are to:

- spend more than 3% on quality – this leads to a less efficient and competitive organisation, and makes the quality function more intrusive
- find alternative ways of providing quality management for 3% of staff costs.

One solution that has worked, preserving both benefits and budget, is to create regular quality management meetings rather than a separate quality section. This uses the 3% of staff time by having everyone involved contribute. These meetings send minutes directly to senior management, providing the independent channel required by ISO9000.

1.9 Stability

One measurement which does seem to be a significant indicator of the level of communication between ITSM and others is the stability of the organisation. Low rates of business change imply a low interaction rate between the IT and business domains. This in turn will affect the relative importance of reactive and proactive processes, the way in which ITIL guidance is best introduced and the benefits realisable.

While we hear much of the high rate of change in the modern business world, this dynamic nature is not universal.

In practical terms, stability is reflected in the number of:

■ reported incidents

■ requests for change

■ contacts with external suppliers and maintainers.

1.9.1   The significance of stability considerations

The stability of an organisation's use of services will influence the relative size of the IT organisation and the overall organisation. Figure 1.4 shows the different scenarios which arise from combining stability (the number of communications with others) with infrastructure size (hardware, software and number of customers). Some volatile organisations have low stability, and therefore a particular need for more intensive IT Service Management.

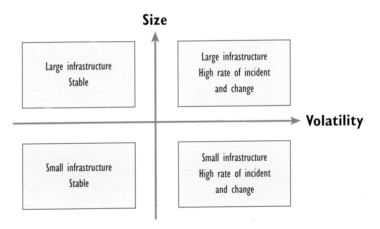

Figure 1.4 Where you might expect to find small IT organisations

The bottom-right quadrant

The primary focus for this book is in the bottom-right quadrant: a small, dynamic ITSM organisation.

The left quadrants

In both left quadrants, stability is the major characteristic. There may be more than one reason why an IT organisation finds itself in this position. It could:

■ have earned stability by tailoring the IT service to user needs

■ be supporting a static customer base

■ have budget and funding issues that are inhibiting change and growth.

There may be other reasons, some of which imply an awareness of ITSM, and others that do not.

Whatever the reason for the stability, it could change very rapidly due to external influences. Being aware of ITSM will always be of benefit to an IT organisation, whatever its size. But unless that change takes place, ITSM is probably not an area that would justify specific process improvement investment; rather such issues would be addressed over longer time periods through standard process review cycles.

In the lower-left quadrant, the organisation is unlikely to have a significant focus on IT. In the smallest stable organisations IT services will be simple, taken as given and relatively low cost. In the upper-left quadrant, the larger size of the overall organisation will make the IT spend more significant, but the stability will permit delivery of the IT services via a small IT organisation.

Top-right quadrant

This type of organisation is the traditional target of the mainstream ITIL guidance.

2 ESTABLISHING ITSM IN SMALL IT ORGANISATIONS

IT Service Management is just as important in small organisations as in larger ones. In today's environment most organisations rely upon relevant and affordable IT support to function. Indeed for many small organisations looking to compete in competitive markets or deliver public sector requirements against tight budget restrictions, IT support is increasingly critical.

In many sectors, IT is moving away from a responsive supporting role towards one of innovations and idea generation for the business. A good example of this is the retail business where IT-generated and IT-based innovations are driving the industry forward. Specific examples from the last 15 years or so range from barcode scanning driving marketing concepts such as 'Buy one get one free' and targeted marketing via data collection through loyalty cards, through to web-based services to customers via interactive electronic trading without the need for sales staff. Many small organisations are, as a business, aiming to exploit new niches in their industry sector, or even create new sectors (or sub-sectors within them at least) such as online gambling and the personal nostalgia business, which can exist only in a web-enabled world.

The IT services supporting innovative new businesses need to be innovative themselves, not just in terms of original solutions to articulated business requirements, but also by feeding into the business opportunities that came into existence due to advances in technology and IT support.

The complexity of IT is not restricted to large organisations. The small IT organisation may need to be just as complex to meet its aims to provide a comprehensive service, and will be challenged further by limited resources and the need to extend its influence beyond the IT department into the rest of the business. A necessary part of ITSM in small organisations will involve creative resourcing using outsiders.

2.1 Setting strategy

Any organisation that intends to have IT services which deliver business benefits will require an IT strategy that is related to the business strategy. The need for a hierarchical approach to strategy, moving from business strategy through IT approach and on to technical considerations, has been well established, and relative size does not affect the argument. Certainly, a strategy for IT services can exist in isolation, but must depend upon the business targets and expectations.

2.1.1 A simple hierarchical view

A simple hierarchical strategy starts with the business strategy of the organisation as a whole (see Figure 2.1). This strategy may in turn be driven by external influences – for example, government organisations will ultimately be driven by political goals and public demands, and utility providers may find strategy reflects current and proposed legislation. The business strategy sets out how business goals and objectives are to be achieved. The ITSM and IT strategies then support these objectives in a direct line relationship. Since it is the services (IT and otherwise) that directly support the business, the business services strategy will be derived directly from the business strategy, with an ITSM strategy either derived from that, or more likely in smaller organisations, forming an element of it. In today's IT-dominated environments the ITSM element may comprise the majority part of any broader business services strategy. The IT strategy, addressing the technological approach of the organisation, will be derived from the service requirements, and in practice will form an input to the organisation's capacity and availability planning.

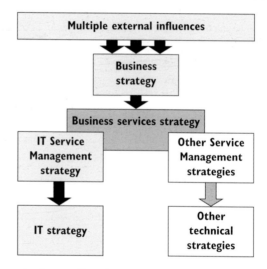

Figure 2.1 A simple example of strategy hierarchy

In large organisations, formal communication channels between the organisation's various divisions mean that this kind of simple view is more or less valid for everyday use.

2.1.2 A more complex view

However, in an age where information systems are pervasive, a simple hierarchical strategy can hide a number of other strategies which will influence IT services. Particularly in smaller organisations, where IT staff are closer to the business users, the true picture is not so much one of direct line departmental relationships, but is instead one of multiple overlapping work groups throughout the organisation (see Figure 2.2). Creating an ITSM strategy in this situation may well require a broader awareness and a more flexible view than that implied by the simple hierarchical model.

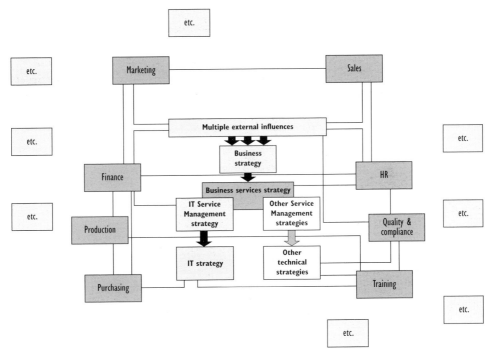

Figure 2.2 Complex interactions

These complex interactions are further influenced by other factors such as:

- the volatility of the market
- the nature of the business
- the attitude of managers.

Small IT organisations need to be aware of all facets of these interactions. Fortunately, in many cases, small size makes it more practical to do this.

The strategies which various parts of the organisation develop will vary in their formality. The current trend seems increasingly towards less formally defined strategies for the medium and long term, as users' empowerment and the volatility of business circumstances increase.

2.1.3   Implications of the business strategy for ITSM

Deciding what services to offer depends on what the business is likely to need in the future. The business strategy should give a clue to this – if it does not, or if there is no formal strategy, the IT organisation should put its own options to senior management about finding a direction for the service.

Strategic issues which will affect the ITSM strategy include:

- new relationships with customers, leading to the need to collect and analyse information in new ways
- changing demands for management information
- customer expectations
- changes in the organisational structure or culture which require new IT capabilities
- moves into new areas of business (forced or voluntary) which need new or changed methods of IT-based support
- changes in business processes (for example, imposed by legislation such as Sarbanes-Oxley or an internal re-engineering exercise) which require a different level or type of IT support
- changes in the existing market or fiscal forecasts which might have an impact on budgeting levels.

2.1.4   Resourcing the ITSM strategy

Small organisations rarely have the internal resources to cover as wide a range of services as larger ones, and fewer people means having less cover in specialist areas. The ITSM strategy recognises this by ensuring that essential services are available in-house, with perhaps a few specialisms as well. Other specialist tasks are subcontracted or outsourced, and business operations themselves can be encouraged to take on some tasks.

Deciding which specialisms to support in-house is likely to depend on:

- what skills and resources are needed
- what skills and resources exist in-house
- how important specified skills are to the organisation (defined by assessing the risk of not having the skill instantly available when it is needed)
- the cost of buying in skills compared with developing them in-house
- the length of time for which the skills will be required
- the availability and reputation of third-party specialists locally.

Using this kind of logic, it is possible to build up a flexible resource base to support appropriate strategies. In practice, many organisations will already be doing this in an ad hoc and unrepeatable fashion, so many ITSM functions will already exist to some extent.

The objective is to eliminate the ad hoc nature of resourcing and to plan the fit-for-purpose resource strategy that aligns with the business need for specialists. It involves examining the current practices, looking for risks and exposures within them (times when the lack of resources and/or specialties have hampered business objectives) and developing a strategy to mitigate these risks.

2.1.5   Developing the ITSM plan

The cycle of planning, from a business plan through the hierarchy of strategies, needs to involve a two-way flow of information before the plans can be finalised. The business plan defines business objectives for the planning period, then the ITSM plans feed back any opportunities or constraints from the world of IT and assigns priorities to competing activities. The planning cycle will address how the organisation will move towards its vision and measure progress against agreed objectives and key performance indicators (KPIs).

2.1.6   Skills constraints

In a small IT organisation feedback to the business plan is especially important because there are likely to be constraints, the effects of which are likely to be more severe than they might be in a larger installation. These constraints are typically due to:

- *available skills* – how well the organisation can support any proposed solutions
- *analysing available skills* – skills which affect business and ITSM plans include knowledge of the business and ability to work with users, as well as knowledge of existing IT systems and the technology in use.

Since people in a small organisation usually fulfil more than one role, ITSM plans should include training. Although this will be mostly on the job, time still needs to be reserved for it. Forward planning estimates should incorporate a target training figure, which can then be monitored using any effort-recording system in use. Failure to identify the need for training and its costs generates false understandings of the costs of delivering services and of replacing staff.

One important area for training is the techniques of skills and knowledge transfer. This will reduce reliance on individuals and is an essential form of insurance against loss of key skills. Learning from others is effective but depends on the ability to convey knowledge; this skill should be recognised, recorded and enhanced where necessary. Formal recognition of passing along skills and knowledge, for example, by documenting it in job descriptions, is important in allowing experienced staff to justify time spent in preparing for and sharing their knowledge. It also reinforces the need to spread knowledge, rather than permitting individuals to build up their reputation based on retained information.

Because of these constraints, the ITSM plan needs to assign priorities. In a small IT unit, as in any other, the key priority must always be to meet business aims and objectives.

2.1.7 Developing support

The demand for support, as well as for software and hardware, is much greater when IT systems are distributed around more than one site, even if the architecture supporting them is simple.

Much of this extra demand can be met by using layered support and appointing users as local systems administrators (LSAs). The LSAs should take on much of the day-to-day running of local systems. It is important to account for the cost of LSA support activities even though they may not appear in the IT organisation's budget. This should be recognised and included in the full cost of IT services to the organisation. This cost needs to appear in any consideration of alternative sourcing, including how the work would be delivered in the alternatives being considered – for example, retained within the user community, included in an outsourcing arrangement, transferred to central support.

2.1.8 Agreeing and delivering the IT service

For any ITSM function, the answer to the key question 'What am I in business *for?*' is 'To provide a service to the organisation'. In order to ask the question properly and deliver the services, service providers (in any size of organisation) must be able to identify and communicate with their customers. Successful communication will rest upon common understanding, especially IT's understanding of the Business Perspective, concepts set out in the ITIL book of that name.

This primary responsibility does not depend on the size of the IT organisation. However, some aspects of agreeing and delivering the service are likely to be different in small IT organisations. Examples include:

- relative ease of contacting the responsible customer in smaller and simpler organisations
- closer relationship to core business processes
- speed of delivery and feedback
- ability to implement improvements faster.

2.1.9 Assigning priorities

Any organisation without access to infinite funds (i.e. every organisation) will have more potentially useful tasks to undertake than they can successfully deal with. The informality and closer collaboration in small organisations can make it harder to say 'No', yet by taking on too many commitments and obligations, the result is usually inadequate service quality, overstretched staff, missed deadlines etc. Therefore it is crucially important for effective prioritisation to be an element of the planning process. In a small IT organisation, as in any other, the key priority must always be to meet business aims and objectives.

It is important to remember that current services and equipment are actually delivering business benefits now; as a result, supporting the current infrastructure must take priority over plans for replacement. And common sense suggests that an organisation which cannot support its current practices is unlikely to be successful with enhancements to them. All plans must reflect the accepted priorities of the work done by the organisation or for which the organisation is responsible.

Planning needs to be comprehensive and take due consideration of all elements, including the internal politics of the organisation. However, a simplistic beginning is a good start that can be expanded. Such a simplistic start includes:

- supporting existing IT systems and software packages
- supporting users, for example, with Service Desk and problem-solving facilities
- buying in any packages which are needed
- managing subcontracted work
- managing custom development work.

A common error among IT organisations in setting priorities is being too concerned with protecting against errors at the expense of providing benefits.

> *Removing all the possible causes of failure does not automatically deliver success.*
>
> Paul Herzlich

Users will often tolerate problems with a service if it still helps them with their work and brings positive business benefits.

A relevant analogy here is car ownership. No matter how well matched a car is to someone's needs, the owner will be able to find something about it they dislike. This will not prevent them from using the car, nor from a repeat purchase of the same model. What is important to the driver is what the car does do, rather than what it doesn't. The same is true in ITSM.

Applying this model to ITSM can help allocate restricted resources to multiple tasks. At its simplest, the process involves:

- identifying all the tasks for which the organisation is responsible
- establishing what resources are required for each, typically expressed in working weeks per financial year
- listing tasks in priority order, with the resources they will need
- counting down the resources column until the total reaches the resources available
- drawing a line here – this represents the work that can be done.

If there are tasks below the line which are vital, a new solution must be found. Which are the 'vital few' tasks needs to be understood by both IT and customer.

In order to be valid, this assessment does not have to be carried out in great detail – most of the benefit (that is, a picture of what *is* actually possible) will come from a quick, broad-brush approach. However, the process is inevitably more complicated than it seems at first sight because:

- *The process is iterative* – the impact of not doing tasks which initially lie below the line often requires a rethink of priorities
- *Priorities are influenced by customers* – customers may be willing to fund some tasks and not others, either directly if there is a charging system, or indirectly through approval at financial committees. Customer opinions in these circumstances are not always easy to predict
- *Resources may not be evenly spread* – an ITSM organisation may find itself with apparently spare resources but with too much work for the only people capable of doing it.

To reinforce this thought, we must drive choices through consideration of what would actively improve performance of the organisation. And that hinges upon establishing and maintaining working relationships so that understanding can be obtained.

2.1.10 Relationships with customers

The service must keep its customers happy and respond to their needs. This means knowing who they are, whether they are internal or a mixture of internal and external, what they want and what they need. This also means knowing how to prioritise their demands. ITSM should be more than a passive instrument and should use ways of adding value to customer service without overstretching its resources. For example:

- the Service Desk knows where local services can be found outside the organisation and can give advice to customers about available options
- ITSM can communicate to customers:
  - about the different things they want, itemising those they can have
  - what the priorities for service provision are (internally or by other means such as cross-service agreements)
  - its performance against agreed service levels
- customers can make suggestions for improving the service, which are noted and taken up where possible.

2.1.11 Documenting and supporting the service

The size of an ITSM organisation is not likely to make any major difference to the need to be clear about the precise services offered. The basic principles apply:

- knowing which services ITSM is responsible for supplying and supporting
- defining, so far as is reasonable, the levels of service required
- ensuring that both supplier and customer share the same view of the service.

2.1.12 Service Level Agreements

Service level requirements, expressed in terms which are comprehensible to customers, are documented and monitored in Service Level Agreements (SLAs).

The IT organisation is always responsible for meeting performance goals in SLAs, subject only to customers fulfilling their obligations. Parts of the service may be provided by consultants, subcontractors or other parts of the organisation (for example, network support, application maintenance or office services). The Service Level Management function must also make sure that the requirements within the SLAs are supported by underpinning contracts. Figure 2.3 shows the concept of a 'waterline'; activities below the line are for ITSM to deal with. The customer in turn relies on ITSM to deliver the service efficiently, economically and reliably.

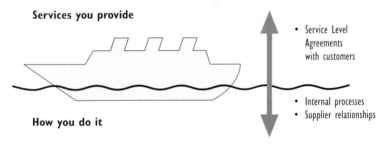

Figure 2.3 The waterline

2.1.13 Relationships with suppliers

Relationships with suppliers often play an important part in providing an effective service. The formal aspect of the relationship with suppliers (both internal and external) is not enough, however essential it is. Small organisations generally depend on suppliers' goodwill and must cultivate it, although without being subservient and remembering who is paying whom for the service and products.

Building a good relationship means:

- providing suppliers or subcontractors with the right information for the job, even beyond the demands of the contract
- listening to suggestions constructively and acting on them, unless they cause problems with the service
- sharing knowledge of the service fully so that suppliers know what to aim for
- recommending suppliers to others if they do a good job and, in return,

expecting them to provide excellent service and product leadership, even beyond the formal demands of the contract.

The contract acts as an assurance that there is, as a last resort, a way of resolving disputes, for use only when all other avenues are closed. It can be useful to document the non-contractual relationship as well; this ensures a common understanding of requirements, procedures and so on. (This might be called a working practices document.)

2.1.14 Documentation

If suppliers are to work with forms, guides, practices and conventions, then, where practicable, it may be beneficial to involve them in producing and especially in maintaining them. Suppliers are likely to have wide experience of different approaches based upon experience with several customers, and will have useful views to consider.

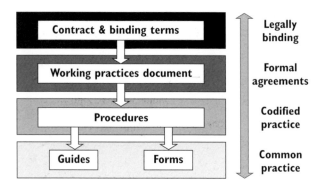

Figure 2.4 Documentation hierarchy

It is worthwhile documenting less tangible aspects of the contract too, such as ideas and ideals. Even though suppliers can only promise to try to fulfil them, writing them down provides both sides with an agreed basis of intention, stability and common language.

The need for documentation applies equally to any mutually beneficial agreements made with any other organisations. A real danger here is to be too informal, relying on good will between individuals who may leave at short notice. Any such agreements should be put on a firm basis with a contract expressing the requirements of the SLA(s), just as for a supplier or subcontractor. Successful relationships of this kind are not common; they rely on two or more organisations having a sufficiently similar approach to an aspect of ITSM to be able to work together for a common benefit.

Circumstances which might encourage their use include:

■ organisations with similar but non-competing objectives, such as government departments

■ situations where joining together creates buying power for things such as consumables, hardware or consultancy.

Example

One organisation, having established a new single-source hardware maintenance contract, spent considerable time devising a control procedure. This procedure used newly designed, multiple-copy forms, and laid down authorities for approval and constraints upon the engineer's authority.

When the contract was in place, it transpired that the supplier's own in-house procedures and paperwork, built upon years of experience, were easier to understand, more comprehensive and cheaper to operate. Pride dictated that the new, cumbersome procedure was used, until the suppliers asked for extra money to compensate for the extra time and effort their staff needed to use it!

2.1.15 Organising the organisation to meet service goals

The way responsibilities are assigned in the organisation should support its service provision in three ways:

- One person should ultimately be accountable for each service, no matter who contributes to providing it
- The process by which services are delivered should have the minimum of handovers across the organisation and no unnecessary steps. Handovers can be eliminated by reorganising functions and processes at the same time (organising ITIL functions in small organisations is dealt with later in this guide (see Chapter 4))
- Similar work should be passed to the same skills groups, making the most of people's abilities and experience (the same knowledge, skills, experience; similar data and results; triggered by the same event with the same timing).

Sometimes these responsibilities, particularly the second and third, are contradictory. Nonetheless, the organisation should work in such a way as to reconcile them as well as possible. An important part of organising efficiently is ruthlessly eliminating unnecessary work – if a task does not contribute directly to the service, it should be eliminated.

Prime candidates for elimination are tasks which:

- are generated by unnecessary steps in the process
- are designed for recording data which is simply retained, never to be used again
- don't contribute to fulfilling SLAs (it may, of course, transpire on investigation that the steps contribute towards something that *should* be covered – in which case, change the SLA, in discussion with the customer).

Within a small ITSM organisation, there will not be spare capacity to carry unnecessary tasks and their profile should be higher, making them more easily identifiable.

2.2   Extending Service Management beyond IT

ITSM is well positioned to offer more than an IT support service alone. ITSM processes require Service Management, and these skills can be used to help with the support and delivery of other services, such as office services, project management, training and personnel. ITSM can act as a channel for delivering a whole range of business support to the user, including helping customers who are developing their own services within a user department.

Additionally, in industries that are specifically focused on providing services as a final product, these same skills can be used throughout the organisation. In government sector organisations or other service-oriented industries some of the concepts of ITSM can be used to improve the levels of service provided to the customer or to the market.

By combining the Service Management of a number of business functions, both the customer and the organisation as a whole stand to benefit from:

- economies of scale
- consistency across a wide range of customer concerns
- a better use of customer-facing staff and their particular skills.

Targeting a wider area than IT services means that much more of the business benefits from the Service Management processes. In turn, this strengthens the case for expenditure on software tools, staff training and change. For many organisations, broadening the base of those who benefit is a vital element of the ITSM cost-benefit equation.

In small organisations, the IT function is often well placed to extend its services to areas where its expertise, experience and resources are relevant. This requires no grand plan: it can happen as opportunities present themselves. Perhaps a service offered to one part of the business can be used (in a different way) by others – new, creative uses for a service are always useful. Or perhaps the skills of the IT organisation can be used to help other parts of the business improve their own performance. If time is available, people can be released to help train others; perhaps staff from other business areas can be seconded to ITSM to learn and, at the same time, help the IT organisation. This can be demonstrated by considering extending:

- the Service Desk
- Service Level Management.

2.2.1   Extending the Service Desk function

An IT Service Desk provides a single point of contact for users to report IT incidents of any kind. This means that users have a familiar and easily reached contact point whether the problem is software, hardware, telecommunications, documentation or training. Users do not have to be able to decide what their issue is before they can get appropriate help.

But the Service Desk does not have to be limited to IT. With IT pervasive in all elements of business, users are often unsure if their issues are caused by IT or something else, or if the business has a request for services that are IT or non-IT in nature. Users can be confused about whom to contact, resulting in delays in getting issues sorted out.

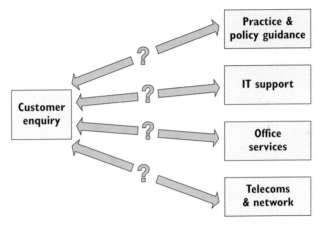

Figure 2.5 Situation with independent support services

Figure 2.5 shows a situation with independent support services. This can be improved by expanding the scope of the Service Desk to receive and log all incidents and service requests that affect the user, whatever their cause (see Figure 2.6). The user then knows where to call for help in case of difficulty. Clearly users benefit, but ITSM also benefits because:

- the wider service means economies of scale, and may mean full-time staff for the Service Desk, resulting in:
    - easier coverage of the shift
    - back-up for staff absence
    - more justification for investing in support tools
    - ability to identify IT-related consequences from seemingly non-IT incidents or requests
- all incidents and requests are logged, making it much less likely that non-IT solutions are applied to incidents and errors that are more easily solved by IT, and vice versa
- the IT organisation becomes more familiar with the rest of the business.

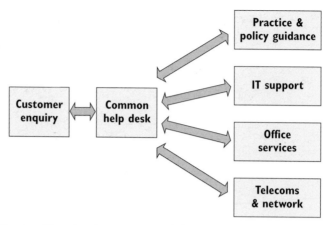

Figure 2.6 Situation with combined support

This logic applies to all the stages within the cycle of reporting, investigating and resolving customer concerns – that is, the Service Support functions within the ITIL context.

2.2.2   Extending Service Level Management

There is nothing in the concepts of identifying, documenting and agreeing details of a service that is unique to IT. SLAs are relevant elsewhere in the organisation, for example in:

- personnel services to staff and business sections
- library or document management services.

The IT organisation is well placed to advise on how to introduce SLAs, but it does not have a monopoly on customer service. This should be a two-way flow of ideas, with good examples of Service Management in non-IT areas too. Although the received wisdom is that Service Level Management (SLM) rests upon the formal documentation and monitoring of SLAs, in many small organisations, much of the SLM process can be seen in a more informal fashion – resting upon people-to-people relationships.

As well as extending the SLM/SLA concept into non-IT services, this conceptual expansion can also help the business by allowing the identification of 'larger' services within which IT plays a significant role. This can involve other, non-IT service providers upon whom the business service depends and gives to the customer a single focus for support of their own business process.

Working with customers and other providers to build a service catalogue that actually documents a genuine customer view of services can greatly assist IT's ability to maximise benefit by working with other service providers to improve business-oriented (rather than IT-oriented) performance metrics.

Example

The internal IT service provider in a bank was seeking service improvement in response to its customers' demands for faster turnaround of applications for credit cards. In setting up SLAs to assist with measuring success, it became clear that the service started when the completed form was received in the mailroom, and ended when the end-customer received a new credit card in the mail. Previously, IT had seen the service as beginning when the completed form was scanned, and ending when approval was granted. The IT people were already beginning to focus on faster repair times for hardware failures and increasing resilience – high-cost remedies that might have improved the IT service by 10% and the overall service by 5%. Taking a view of the broader service, improvements in the ingoing and outgoing mailrooms were able to deliver a 20% improvement at minimal cost.

2.3 Using external skills

IT organisations use external resources to make sure they have all the right skills for ITSM, as most specialised skills will be needed for only a small percentage of the time, making it impractical and uneconomic to develop them in-house.

In a small organisation, expenditure on external skills is likely to be a significant cost – higher than for a large organisation, where it becomes more feasible to develop in-house skills, or where bought-in skills are used in larger chunks at cheaper rates. While all small organisations are likely to have to buy in skills, very small organisations will be buying in both skills and resources since they will have neither the numbers to cope with peaks of work nor the breadth of experience.

Consultancy is often an essential element of implementing new ITSM functions. It offers invaluable experienced support for the set-up processes, which by their nature create one-off peaks of work.

There are two options for obtaining third-party skills. The difference lies in who takes responsibility for day-to-day control. The key is often the extent to which the service can be bounded and separated:

- *Contracting out* – this takes place when there is a clearly defined need for a particular end product or service. A specification for the product or service is agreed, and the supplier has responsibility for managing and delivering it
- *Buying in* – this refers to situations where temporary resources are needed, or

where a particular skill is used occasionally but regularly. Day-to-day control remains with ITSM, who are usually charged on the basis of time supplied. This provides more control and integration, but of course the organisation still has to find the resources to manage it.

2.3.1   Skills transfer

Whether services are contracted out or bought in, it is often important for a skills transfer to take place from external sources to in-house staff.

If it is done correctly, this skills transfer can:

- reduce the need for (as much) bought-in resource in future similar circumstances
- clarify and simplify future discussions with external specialists (due, in part at least, to an understanding of the terms and principles involved)
- improve staff morale by broadening individuals' skills and understanding.

Problems with skills transfers can be that they:

- take up so much time and effort that they get in the way of the job and/or result in unforeseen extra expenditure
- are pursued because staff members are interested solely for their own sakes (that is, they are succumbing to technical curiosity or believe it will increase their own marketability)
- are not used often enough once learned to be retained, which can result in repeated training and additional costs in delays of service and resources used.

It is not necessarily efficient to learn from external expertise in every situation, unless that knowledge will be useful. Sufficient awareness to judge the quality of the external service is almost always useful, but deeper levels of skill will only become beneficial if they ease the delivery of the bought-in service or if they are likely to lead towards the ability to deliver in the future using less external resources.

Part of the difficulty is that staff may be personally interested in learning and understanding skills that will not directly benefit the organisation. For many good staff, the possibility of deeper understanding and broadening of their own skills is attractive enough to take precedence over delivering their everyday job, which may be less fascinating by comparison.

2.3.2   Cross-servicing

Two IT organisations in the same town or district with a similar IT infrastructure and some common needs may decide that they can do a better job for their users by providing each other with particular services. Examples of cross-servicing might include:

- off-site storage
- providing facilities for hardware maintenance, such as engineers' stores and accommodation
- specialist support skills that one may provide to the other on a reciprocal basis.

2.3.3 Recommendations for working with external suppliers

Organisations should consider using external suppliers if:

- they have to invest a great deal of effort or skills to maintain specialist services; in this case they should stick to basic, common services
- the alternative is employing people who can only do one specialised job which is rarely needed.

If work does go out to external suppliers, contracts must reflect the service agreements the IT organisation has signed with the business. Contracts must include all aspects of standards and legislation which are needed to deliver the services concerned.

2.4 Developing the service

ITSM can do much more than run computers. As we have seen, it should also support the organisation's business objectives. To do this, it will:

- provide a business service
- add more value to the business as a whole
- establish connections through the business so that if the IT organisation doesn't know the answer, it knows who does and, in a full sense, provides information.

But the wide choice of services the IT organisation could supply is constrained by limited resources. How should the choice be made?

The core service is providing IT services and, via these, support to the business. Without this, the organisation will not have a firm foundation of satisfactory performance. SLAs should start from here.

2.4.1 Service improvement

It may be that resources are so tight that nothing else is possible, though this seems unlikely. In any case, plans should always assume that existing resources of all kinds can be better used. Without such pressure there is little tangible incentive to improve performance, resulting in missed opportunities. Additionally, organisations that keep missing opportunities are less likely to survive.

Usually there are ways to get better results:

- parts of internal processes – steps, forms, files and so on – can be eliminated, thus reducing the workload

- some services can be prioritised by referring to existing business, ITSM and IT plans (see Section 2.1) – this is a two-way process since ITSM and IT plans should be made with reference to constraints of staff and skills.

These positive ways of focusing the service should help to balance resource constraints.

Many techniques and methods exist to help professionals improve the processes through which they deliver services. Some of these require considerable investment in training and qualification; others are better suited to smaller organisations which have neither significant funds for training nor long time frames for implementation. One illustrative example of an approach well suited to small organisations is the 'Lean Philosophy', which can be valuable in boosting performance. Although initially developed within and for a production environment, focusing as it does on eliminating waste, improving speed and encouraging innovation, it is equally applicable to the delivery of improved services.[1]

The practical judge of ITSM is customer perception, which leads ultimately to business success. So ITSM must be continually aware of it, and also of the pressures customers face, their attitudes and their concerns. ITSM should take every opportunity to add value over and above the core services it provides and remain, as much as possible, aware of business trends.

2.4.2 Front-line knowledge

Those most likely to be in touch with the individuals actually using services are often the more junior people, who, for instance, staff the front-line Service Desk, audit assets and so on. Their proximity to users can be a very useful source of contacts and ideas.

Communication between customers (typically business managers of staff actually using the service) and IT services managers, such as negotiating SLAs, is sensible and valid. However, those involved may well be out of touch with everyday reality. In the informal approaches more common in smaller organisations, it can be very important to discover and take note of how services and equipment are *actually* used, and indeed what is normal business practice, not just what is correctly documented business process. To this end, input to planning and service improvement from more junior staff is valuable, and often more practically achieved within the smaller groups of small organisations.

---

1 Information on the 'Lean Philosophy' from the Lean Institute, www.lean.org

2.5 ITSM and the IT infrastructure

Decisions about planning an IT infrastructure are strategic and affect the whole organisation, not just ITSM. Thus the most ITSM can hope to do is to influence these strategic decisions.

Aspects of IT infrastructure planning which have a major influence on ITSM include:

- *Minimum spread* – this means making a *strategic architectural choice* very early, and minimising variation so far as is consistent with delivering the required levels of service to customers

- *Reliability, maintainability and serviceability* – Service Delivery depends on locally available support. If the organisation cannot tackle much that is complex, a good call-out response time is important

- *Cost* – even today, the IT architecture may well need to perform over a long time period, so whole lifecycle costs need to be considered. Features which influence cost include:
  - charges for maintenance
  - ease of maintenance
  - expected failure rates
  - durability and maintainability of software
  - depreciation costs and possible resale values
  - upgrade ability – will it be obsolete after 24 months or can it be upgraded?

3 MANAGING A SMALL IT ORGANISATION

The principles involved in managing an IT organisation are more or less the same, regardless of size. However, making sure that small organisations are organised to carry out all the services required of them, and making sure they have the skills to do so, can present some particular management problems.

3.1 Adopting a hands-on approach

The major difference in a small organisation is that managers will need a much more hands-on approach to data gathering, especially the compilation of appropriate information.

Some managers might see this as a problem, but there are advantages:

- proximity to the work means managers have a better understanding of the real needs and wants of customers and IT staff
- managers stay closely in touch with staff and the day-to-day issues affecting the organisation
- there is less likelihood of data gathering for the sake of it
- management is more flexible and changes of practice are easier to implement.

3.1.1 Keeping time records

One particular aspect of a hands-on approach to management is knowing how people spend their time. This takes effort, but it is justifiable in specific circumstances. It is, however, more useful to concentrate on recording outputs (i.e. results) rather than resources consumed (i.e. time), and to encourage staff to improve estimating by recording time personally. Time is then planned on the basis of a 'full shop', with everyone fully occupied and their commitments entered in the diary of activity for the organisation.

Good ITSM tools can help remove the burden of time tracking by using the lifecycle tracking features from Service Management. For example, logging the time elapsed from the detection of an incident mapped against who is providing the service, will, over time, provide trends of how time is being spent. There are endless possibilities here to evaluate options for improving time management. The use of the Service Desk logging of activities will help this effort.

3.2 Managing tasks

Once the IT organisation has defined the services it can provide in response to the ITSM plan and the Service Level Agreements (SLAs), it can draw up a list of tasks it must carry out. The points to consider are:

- how tasks should be organised and managed
- which tasks fit naturally together
- the skill mix needed to perform the tasks
- the compromises which can be made to meet the goal of matching like tasks with like skills.

3.2.1 Matching skills and tasks

In the search for quality, management effort is traditionally directed towards the processes underlying service or product delivery. This is amply demonstrated by the high profile of quality management initiatives such as ISO9000. However, in reality, delivered quality is often more a matter of how well people's skills match those needed by the job: there may be considerable potential for improving quality by matching skills in this way. In a small organisation, it is both feasible and desirable to carry out an audit of skills.

3.2.2 Techniques for assessing skills and requirements

In order to match staff skills and job requirements, separate assessments are needed of:

- the skills available
- the skills needed to carry out the organisation's tasks.

Simple techniques exist for carrying out these assessments at a broad-brush level – the more sophisticated personality-profiling tests should be avoided by anyone not skilled in their interpretation.

Techniques for assessment might consist of:

- Each person completing a questionnaire designed to reveal features of their personality and their work preferences
- Analysing each job to establish what particular skills or personality features it requires. (This is also a good opportunity to ask the question 'Do we still need to do this job at all?' – probably best expressed as 'What would be the consequences if this were not done?')
- Matching people to jobs (some 'management' interpretation of people's self-assessment might well be necessary).

Making a best-fit match between people and jobs might involve:

- retraining people for jobs better suited to their skills and preferences
- re-allocating staff to different departments within the organisation
- restructuring jobs so that all elements can be carried out efficiently by one person (for example, making sure elements requiring a methodical approach are not mixed with those requiring inspirational thinking).

Even a small improvement in matching skills is likely to be worthwhile in terms of improved performance and staff morale. An exercise which detects a task that would be better dealt with by external resources can release internal staff for tasks they are skilled in. Indeed, if done, skill matching can significantly increase job satisfaction and hence staff retention. The costs of staff turnover are disproportionately high in small organisations and can be a significant factor in meeting economic targets and efficiency levels. A perfect fit is never possible, but people will respond positively to attempts to find jobs which suit them.

3.3 Managing technology

IT organisations, even small ones, may end up with infrastructure components from a variety of sources. This introduces complications for:

- *spares* – a wide range has to be available
- *supplier and maintenance arrangements* – apart from the complications of having a number of arrangements, suppliers can be less loyal or motivated with only a small part of the business and competition on the same site
- *staff knowledge* – with limited people, chances of someone knowing something about every part of the infrastructure are reduced
- *problem solving* – this is much more complex with a variety of components
- *upgrade paths* – a change in one area will mean complex adjustments throughout the infrastructure.

Obviously it is best not to have such a mix of infrastructure components. Often, however, there is no alternative in the short term. The medium- to long-term solution is to reduce the variety of infrastructure components. This requires control of IT purchasing, and, while this is a sensible control to vest within IT, it is not always quickly achievable in organisations, especially smaller ones with informal attitudes and/or devolved financial authority. The non-financial arguments for consistency across the infrastructure are valid and sellable but this will take time and effort.

Nonetheless, there are some immediate actions which can be helpful:

- single-source maintenance agreements

- joint maintenance agreements
- managing administration.

3.3.1 Single-source maintenance agreements

It may be possible to pass the whole maintenance support on to a third party who will take responsibility for all the infrastructure components and all the suppliers. This gains leverage, since the third party will have other sites and thus more influence and a higher priority with suppliers. Small organisations should make sure that these advantages are passed on to them if they do make such an agreement.

There are disadvantages, however. The organisation may lose hands-on control. Upgrading may be more complex because the maintenance agreement has to be taken into account. The organisation has to rely on an outsider for critical aspects of the service. Such agreements must be managed through carefully constructed underpinning contracts, drawn down from the agreed SLAs.

3.3.2 Joint maintenance agreements

An alternative is for two or more IT organisations to make a joint maintenance agreement with suppliers. This means keeping control while gaining some leverage. But agreements can be hard to reach, and need good contacts and, above all, close cooperation to work well. Experience shows that this 'cooperative' concept works best where there are common goals for the organisations (for example, government organisations, and security of shared services such as inter-bank transfers). It also usually performs better where one organisation takes the lead in supplier negotiation and relationship management – running a contract by committee is rarely convenient or successful.

3.3.3 Managing administration

All ITSM tasks include an element of administration. It is not restricted to basic tasks such as filing, but covers more general support work, including keeping minutes of meetings, forms and process management, quality system administration and producing management information.

Administration is an essential part of any efficient organisation; it supports and enables progress rather than obstructing it. There are essential ITSM administrative tasks integral to an IT organisation, even a small one.

Experience shows that small organisations need to allocate at least 10% of staff numbers to administration. With less, others have to take the load or leave essential administration undone. Either way the service suffers.

In many organisations, most day-to-day users will be in administrative roles. This opens up considerable opportunities for both the IT organisation and the business, for example:

- appointing full-time or shared administration staff to IT who have current knowledge of the business
- exchanging staff between business and IT organisations, establishing friendly contact between the two environments
- building up a reservoir of IT-literate staff.

An enlightened organisation may well make use of such staff for more than administrative purposes, for example, for establishing the potential or real usability of new or changed services (and not just the IT components).

3.4   Managing information

Any organisation, large or small, needs to manage its activities, and management needs to make decisions and therefore requires information on which to base those decisions. A small organisation, with limited resources, most of whom are required to deliver multiple responsibilities, is unlikely to be able to justify anyone dedicated to developing appropriate management information. It is therefore important that a general understanding of capturing data and condensing it into usable information is instilled in staff.

The temptation, easily succumbed to by technically-oriented specialists in a small organisation, is to capture as much data as possible. This is not constructive for a small organisation which will not have the staff to support the maintenance of that data.

Instead, it needs to be recognised that, however small the organisation, managing data in a way that helps generate information is an activity worthy of resources. Typically, senior IT managers will work with customers, colleagues and suppliers to establish what information they will need in order to manage their IT service provision. Working with their staff and suppliers, they can develop a structure to deliver, update and maintain the data necessary to derive the information and justify the funding for it.

4 A STRUCTURE FOR ITSM IN SMALL IT ORGANISATIONS

The IT services manager within a small IT organisation has to make sure that all tasks are covered with only a small number of staff. In most cases, the number of identified roles within ITSM will be more than the number of people in the organisation.

4.1 Adapting roles

This section looks in detail at how to combine and adapt roles within the confines of a small organisation.

The major influences on how those roles are actually performed include:

- staff attitudes, making possible overlap, cross-function working and mutual support (or interference) between ITIL functions
- restrictions on scope, both because of limitations imposed by staffing and finance, and because the complexity and rigour appropriate for mainstream ITIL functions will not be so necessary.

Additionally there are aspects of ITSM which apply to all sizes of organisation, but which are particularly visible within a small one, where they are also often easier to deal with. Examples include user education and awareness, where a more flexible approach can be taken when dealing with smaller numbers.

In many ways, small IT organisations are in a position to benefit most from increased technology to automate processes, relieving the load on staff. Automation can be a way of offering a full-time process, even when the function itself is only staffed part-time.

4.2 Suggested roles

Each ITSM function can be seen as an assembly of component tasks. ITIL explains how these combine into mainstream ITSM roles. However, this structure needs to be reconsidered for small IT organisations. The structure below suggests one way in which scaling down might be achieved. It is important to build a solution that matches the specific requirements of each organisation. What follows is suggested as a starting point for a 'typical' small organisation for matching actual circumstances and requirements.

The nature of each of these suggested roles is explored in more detail in the next few pages, together with some examples of how the roles might be delivered and matched to the small environment.

4.3   Role 1 – Proactive Problem and Availability Management

At first sight these two areas may seem unrelated – in mainstream ITIL terms, Problem Management is in Service Support and Availability Management is part of Service Delivery. However, they share a commitment to a proactive, forward-looking and inventive approach. In fact, good Availability Management can be said to be reflected by the absence of availability problems – within acceptable cost limits, of course.

Within a small organisation, this is a good example of how to build a job around tasks which require similar skills. If the organisation develops internal applications, then the development staff will have much of the expertise needed to prevent problems, especially software ones, and to manage availability. There should already be close liaison with them for:

- building in good availability
- fixing faults as they occur.

Similarly, network teams, application suppliers and others with relevant skills should be incorporated into virtual problem teams to consider risks and suggest problem minimisation approaches.

ITSM should, however, be aware that final responsibility for these measures must remain with them. If not, there is a very real danger that supporting live services will take second place to the development of new ones.

Many small organisations recognise the importance of Problem Management by assigning a proportion of staff time to it. Problem Management does not have to be a full-time role. IT staff, especially support staff, will have deep knowledge of both the infrastructure and the way the business uses it – this is the major prerequisite for delivering good Problem Management. Combining this with the inevitable peaks and troughs of support work means that there is a potential Problem Management resource available.

A typical approach is to hold a Problem Management meeting regularly, say on every other Tuesday afternoon. The group will consider the current situation, identify the best areas to concentrate resources according to business priorities, and assign top-priority tasks to individuals or teams to work on as time permits. These action items will then be on the agenda to be reported on at the next meeting.

4.4   Role 2 – Incident Management and Service Desk

In small IT organisations, Service Desk staff are more aware of how the organisation operates and can interpret this for their customers.

Where there is a wide diversity of users, either geographically or of specialisms, it makes sense to identify local systems administrators (LSAs) from user staff. Selecting LSAs:

- lightens the load for the ITSM Service Desk

- provides users with someone familiar with their working environment as a first point of contact

- filters out trivial and multiple incidents.

In order to keep an accurate picture of customer concerns and incidents, LSAs should log all the incidents they receive and resolve. This will be more feasible if they have access to the software support tool on which incidents are logged.

In practice, no organisation captures every incident, and the benefits of doing so should not be allowed to outweigh the overheads, nor indeed the benefits of local resolution, be that by formally recognised 'super users', local administrators etc. or by the informal 'local expertise'.

4.4.1   Service Desk codes of conduct

Service Desks see themselves as the single point of contact between customers and IT services; however, business managers and customers see them as the contact point for the whole of the IT organisation. In order to fulfil that role, Service Desks must adopt a code of conduct which specifies:

- never blaming other parts of the IT organisation for any problems

- accepting comments, suggestions and complaints about any aspect of the IT directorate's service, logging them, and channelling them to the right person

- having enough knowledge to understand such calls, or making sure that the customer is contacted by someone else who does.

4.4.2   Coping with a part-time Service Desk role

In a small IT organisation, it will probably not be possible to justify manning the Service Desk full-time. What often happens is that the people responsible for taking Service Desk calls work on other things as well. However, they are then constantly interrupted – the very thing the Service Desk system was designed to avoid. Section 2.2.1 looked at the potential for widening the Service Desk's coverage to provide a business service. Other techniques that may help include:

- *Medical treatment concept* – full Service Desk services are available at set times – that is, 'office hours'; frequently asked questions (FAQs) and emergency contact information are available for the rest of the working day. This at least reduces the level of interruption to IT staff, but it does rely on having understanding customers

- *Using the spare time of Service Desk staff for proactive work* – this might involve:
  - carrying out audits of IT or other assets via telephone calls or remote software
  - notifying users of any new changes or workarounds
  - contacting users to check satisfaction or just to keep in touch
  - updating manuals and documentation – the Service Desk is in a good position to judge users' levels of understanding and comprehension
- *Introducing automation* – this can be done by using intelligent telephone systems that would give callers options, for example:
  - press 2 for news about the current situation (perhaps the network is down and will be restored in 30 minutes, which will explain many users' problems)
  - press 9 to record a message logging your incident which will be dealt with in due course
  - press 0 to talk to someone in an emergency.

Additionally this can be done through the use of web-based technology, via an intranet site where users can get self-help answers to some less complex problems. This can be accomplished through publishing of FAQs and user guides and then educating users on where to find and how to use this new knowledge.

4.4.3   Matching Service Desk processes to need

Procedures should be no more complicated than they need to be and should reflect *customers'* perceptions of incidents and problems, rather than ITSM's. For example, a complex structure of incident classification is neither necessary nor helpful. More intuitive is using three levels of priority, an approach proven over thousands of years in approaches such as categorising the wounded (triage).

How incidents are ranked must reflect their impact upon the business they support, and not ITSM criteria. For example, a broken printer is just a routine incident to IT. However, to the business it could be very serious if important month-end printing was taking place. To make ranking criteria clear, everyday language should be used to describe the priority levels, for example:

Priority level 1   I can't do something important

Priority level 2   Please fix as soon as you can, but I can get on with something else for now

Priority level 3   I can live without it for a while

Organisations increasing their ITSM maturity may choose to have more than three incident categories if they observe that only having three is leading to 'level 2' being used for the vast majority of incidents – where there is a 'middle' level, it can be used no matter what, rather than really trying to determine the actual impact. Alternatively, an awareness campaign to recognise the value of using the full range and categorising properly may be successful in changing behaviour.

4.5   Role 3 – Configuration, Change and Release Management

ITIL strongly recommends the combination of Configuration, Change and Release Management. This is sound and sensible guidance, and even more relevant in smaller organisations because:

- it is inevitable that roles will be combined
- the distinctions between the roles are less defined and responsibility is more likely to flow across process boundaries
- formal release is less likely to be defined; by combining the roles, it is more likely that the key release processes will be addressed.

This combined role can be referred to as the 'greater change' role. It deals with defining the infrastructure configuration and controlling or carrying out changes to it.

This is, in many ways, the counterpoint to Role 1 – Proactive Problem and Availability Management – in that it deals with reactive responsibilities, and is more the back-room job forming the foundation of ITSM, generating and maintaining the accurate basic data without which ITSM cannot perform effectively.

In many small organisations, taking the full ITIL approach to Configuration Management will not be worthwhile – the overheads of establishing and maintaining the configuration links will be too great. However, it is still essential to record assets accurately in some way.

When change requests are received, a small organisation can assess them without the need to appoint a hands-on change manager role, by setting up and documenting appropriate consultation processes instead. Meetings to assess and decide on any debatable change requests and to assign priorities will still be needed, usually chaired by the IT services manager, who would retain process ownership.

If the organisation as a whole has formal change control procedures with which the IT organisation complies, any major changes can be dealt with under them. This has the advantages of:

- making sure that the organisation as a whole is involved in any changes to working practices
- considering the impact of change requests for the business as a whole, not just the IT aspects
- using a single, universally understood approach and a uniform process.

4.6   Role 4 – Finance and Resource Capacity Management

These tasks are so specialist that most small organisations would not normally find it economical to keep them in-house. Organisations have a choice of either spending over the odds or using third-party support: in both cases, in-house work will be needed to carry out the roles on a day-to-day basis. If the necessary skills are not already available in-house, it would be wise to establish whether Finance and Resource Capacity Management are to be done through consultancy, keeping in mind that, however small, any organisation is likely to have internal access to financial expertise. Making use of the organisation's finance department for advice may well be a sensible starting point. Indeed many of the financial aspects of administering a small IT organisation may well be dealt with directly by the finance group.

4.6.1   Finance Management

All organisations need to know what each of their IT services cost. This information allows them to:

- make sound judgements on the financial justification for requests for change and enhancements
- determine whether the service offers value for money, when cost is compared against usage
- identify high-cost services to target for cost reduction
- judge the financial viability of in-house against outsourced service provision.

However, establishing accurate costing is expensive and resource intensive. To keep costs to a minimum, small IT organisations need to establish carefully the degree of accuracy they really need. They must resist the temptation to introduce more complex and expensive schemes. If the point of the scheme is to identify the cost of providing services to customers, most of the information can be derived from a relatively inaccurate system.

The golden rule is keep it simple. Start with basic measures and introduce more detail only when it is justified. Stated simply, without a situation where the lack of sufficiently accurate or detailed financial information causes difficulty in making decisions, there will not be the justification for spending more money on improved financial monitoring.

Once the costing system is up and running, maintaining it will require:

- software monitoring tools
- a staff time-recording system
- an analysis of the measures which have been observed.

4.6.2   Resource Capacity Management

ITIL considers Capacity Management as comprising three elements with a hierarchical relationship. Business Capacity Management rests upon predicting the business situation and has been addressed as an element of planning and strategy in Section 2.1. Without knowing how the business requirements are likely to change, it would be impossible to predict accurately the IT (and other) service usage (Service Capacity Management) and therefore the IT infrastructure required to deliver those services (Resource Capacity Management).

Many small organisations spend a large part of their ITSM resources on supporting office automation software running across networked PCs. There are very few cheap and simple Capacity Management tools and techniques for this – getting by often depends on common sense and feedback from users.

On larger platforms (up to mainframes) all aspects of Capacity Management, such as capacity planning, monitoring hardware usage, tuning systems, establishing and maintaining appropriate reporting, need experts who are skilled in dealing with the particular platform, as well as expensive monitoring software. Even medium-sized to large organisations will probably not invest in this expertise and equipment, since it is only needed for a few weeks each year.

4.7   Role 5 – IT Services Continuity Management

In small organisations, the IT department is probably integrated physically with the rest of the organisation. So, even more than in a larger organisation, it is counter-productive to consider how to recover the IT service in isolation. Any disaster will affect the business as a whole and planning for it should consider business continuity on an organisational level. ITSM must obviously consider its own needs following a disaster, but it should do this as a member of the Business Continuity Management (BCM) team.

Nonetheless there are specific IT aspects that need to be addressed within the overall BCM plan and the IT organisation is responsible for these. If the organisation has centralised IT facilities, then consideration will need to be given to alternatives in the event that they are lost, and, if the BCM plan involved using alternative locations in the event of a disaster to the normal site, the availability of appropriate IT within the new site should be addressed.

Even when the continuity exercise has been outsourced to a specialist third party, day-to-day maintenance of the IT element should fall to the IT organisation. Any significant change to IT provision or working practices could invalidate the plan and should be spotted by the IT organisation beforehand. Effectively what this means is that, however small the IT organisation, they should be a part of any continuity teams across the organisation.

4.8 Role 6 – Service Level Management, Business and Service Capacity Management, Charging and Relationship Management

In the smallest of IT organisations, this role will go with the IT director responsibility, since it includes responsibility for the relationship with the customer and overall service quality, as well as for suggesting and managing future service provision. We have dealt with the need for a strategic approach to IT in Section 2.1.

4.8.1 Service Level Management

With all services, the key to establishing, measuring and delivering the correct level of service is the documented agreement on what is to be provided. This is important, but often difficult to establish in a small environment, where there is likely to be a tradition of informality and providing services in an ad hoc fashion.

Negotiating service levels in the smaller organisation's 'village-type' environment can cause particular problems. The formality required can be undermined because:

- each side knows (or believes it knows) the other side's requirements
- personalities are well known
- bargaining positions have been the subject of extensive informal communication
- there is a culture of 'helping out' and 'doing favours' rather that an obligation to deliver against measurable parameters.

To counteract this, it is especially important that everyone in the IT organisation understands Service Level Management (SLM), what it is for and how it works. They will all, consciously or not, be passing messages to customers. This is effectively requiring a change of culture, or at least a partial change – too much formality and separation will not improve the overall service. It is also very important that everyone in the IT organisation knows who the customers are and who the users are. Since they will most likely be interacting with both groups, from a support perspective, it is important that they understand who does and who does not have the authority to authorise requirements for service.

The person responsible for fronting negotiations with customers is particularly important, since the credibility of SLM will start with the credibility and reputation of that individual. To succeed, negotiators must have:

- *the respect of the IT organisation* – otherwise they will not be able to establish what level of service can be offered in the negotiations
- *authority* – negotiators must be senior enough to be taken seriously and for

their decisions to be acted upon; usually this is determined by grading and pay levels

■ *the respect of the IT organisation's customer.*

4.8.2   Business and Service Capacity Management

Understanding the business strategy sufficiently well to predict the business demands is a task that requires significant business understanding, and is also an essential precursor to even considering the services and resources that will be required. Unless there is relevant and up-to-date business experience within the IT organisation, the best way to achieve this is usually in collaboration with expertise from the business. This can often be achieved with a two- or three-hour meeting. In many small organisations where the IT manager reports to board level or the CEO, it may be solved simply as a session between the IT manager and their manager. These meetings should take place on a sufficiently frequent basis to keep IT in touch with changes in the business goals and objectives.

Management of the services should be relatively 'hands-off' in small organisations but will require some application in terms of:

■ Ensuring sufficient licences of software are available to meet business requirements and, if this is not possible, introducing a mechanism for rationing or prioritising usage

■ Ensuring that new or changed services are sized with sufficient accuracy (not too little so that responses are not predictable, but also not too accurately so that it is too expensive). This cross-over between Service Level Management and Service Capacity Management should benefit from the combination of the roles.

4.8.3   Charging

The relevance of charging is not especially affected by an organisation's size. In many very tiny organisations (for example, two- or three-people partnerships) separation of financial responsibility and benefits is important and justifies the administrative overheads involved. However, whatever the size of organisation, those overheads are significant and should not be embarked upon without sound business justification in terms of the consequential benefits. This consideration is especially important within a small organisation because, while things cost less in small organisations, the percentage of the overall IT spend consumed will be higher since economies of scale are not available, and since measurement and billing software are less likely to be available and are, again, disproportionately expensive for small implementations. If the overall organisation requires internal charging for services the approach should be to deliver no finer level granularity of charging than is essential.

4.8.4   Relationship Management

In smaller organisations, the responsibility for managing relationships with both customers and suppliers will usually be retained by the IT services manager and sits logically with the SLM role. Small organisations are likely to be heavily dependent on one or two key suppliers, not having the size to justify multiple sourcing. Establishment and maintenance of a mutually supportive relationship becomes all the more important in these circumstances. Establishing a meaningful relationship with large suppliers is difficult for small organisations, but typically they will depend on some multinational hardware, as well as software and telecommunications suppliers. Possible aids to the situation rest with collaboration with other, similarly placed small organisations to form a loud enough lobby with large suppliers, or via user groups.

4.9   Vital ITIL

The various elements of ITSM are inexorably entwined, making it very difficult to separate out any one element and implement that as a stand-alone process. Successful ITSM organisations tend to be successful because they have the broad range of ITSM processes in place and working cooperatively.

However, many small organisations have very little in the way of implemented ITSM processes and need some clues on where to start and which processes would be most appropriate to them. In other words which parts of ITIL are *vital* to small organisations?

With the usual caveats already expressed in this book (that suggestions are only suggestions, and that all organisations are different etc.), some generalisations may be useful to immature ITSM initiatives. Experience shows that useful ideas to consider as starting points are:

- service catalogue
- Incident Management
- Configuration Management.

4.9.1   Service catalogue

Until you are aware of the services you support, it will always be difficult to support them. Even at its simplest – a list of the services customers receive from the IT organisation – this is an immensely valuable document and the ideal starting point for a small organisation. Vital considerations are:

- Services must be described in customers' terms and reflect services they can relate to. Examples of appropriate services are 'HR systems', 'e-mail' and 'desktop'. Networks, servers and mainframes are not usually services for this purpose

- Start simply and always involve the business. Begin with a simple list and add more information about each service at a later stage, moving towards more sophisticated catalogues further down the track towards mature ITSM

- Make the catalogue widely available and ensure it is agreed and understood by IT staff as well as customers and users.

4.9.2   Incident Management

Without a central point of contact capturing all incidents, very little constructive to improve the service can be done. Unless you establish what is going wrong, understanding and justifying the correct action is unlikely.

With an effective Service Desk in place, all user concerns can be dealt with and, if incident matching and prioritisation are in place, then:

- Each incident, or more importantly its underlying cause, will be addressed precisely once, i.e. none will be forgotten and several different staff will not tackle the same issue separately, since multiple occurrences can be matched

- The issues that are causing the most business pain will be addressed first. This rests upon assigning a meaningful impact and urgency as each call is reported.

4.9.3   Configuration Management

No small organisation starting from an immature ITSM position is going to introduce full ITIL Configuration Management. Instead a small organisation needs to capture only the data that will be useful in managing the service. Here a sensible starting point is the service catalogue, using the agreed services as the first Configuration Items and identifying components that support them, allowing impact analysis to be applied, both for incident and change assessment.

4.10   Sourcing of ITSM processes

IT services managers will need to identify the best way of carrying out the tasks which support the IT needs of the business. Only a minority of essential ITSM functions are intrinsically better done in-house. Equally though, only a minority are intrinsically better outsourced if the organisation happens to have the right skills to hand.

The options for delivering the various tasks within ITSM can be set out as follows.

- *ITSM provides*
  services that need to be retained in-house and performed by the IT services section

- *ITSM jointly provides*
  services that can be delivered by IT services in partnership with another provider (this may be third party, application development or business organisations)

- *Business provides*
  services that are best supplied by staff within the business function (although the cost may still be seen as part of supporting IT within the organisation)

- *Third party provides*
  services that are best outsourced to external service providers

- *Developer provides*
  services that can be supplied by the application development staff or system procurement staff (which might also be an outsourced function).

This concept and suggested sourcing of ITSM elements is addressed in considerably more detail in Annex A.

Of course, each IT organisation is unique, so although the advice given here applies generally to small IT organisations, there will be exceptions.

Each IT services manager must consider:

- what IT services are dictated by the needs of the business
- constraints applying within the organisation
- skills that will be needed to provide services
- skills available
- the budget.

Figure 4.1 illustrates a logical approach to deciding which tasks should be done within IT services and which should be done elsewhere.

4.10.1 Underlying assumptions

The steps within the algorithm are based upon some underlying assumptions about the organisation and how it interfaces with others.

- The developers or procurers of in-house systems know (and care about) what happens in all stages of the system lifecycle, including the Service Delivery stage. If they do not, they will neither be able nor willing to take responsibility for problem solving and prevention

- There are close links in place with suppliers or maintainers of all the infrastructure elements (particularly network and software components), preferably electronic

- Management reporting and metrics-gathering are automated. Support tools

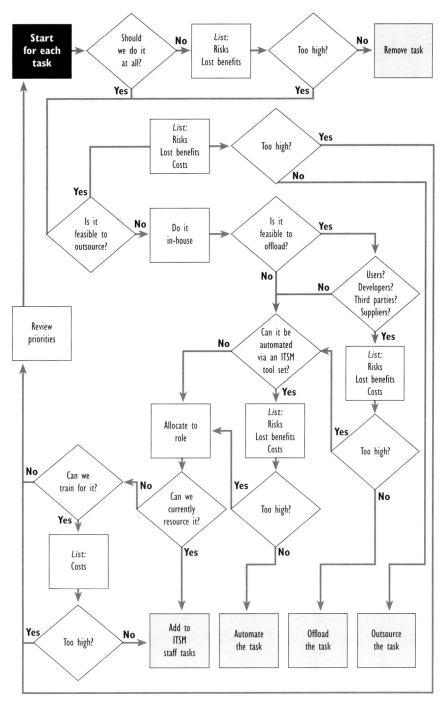

Figure 4.1 Algorithm for deciding what tasks should be done by whom and with what support

help to deal with ad hoc, complex queries and with the production of time-based reports (for example, weekly reports on the status of change requests)

■ Suppliers are committed to implementing initial queries and to providing ongoing support for changes

■ The Service Desk can provide cover for user calls. This can be achieved in either of two ways:

– increasing the breadth of services offered outside IT

– offloading simpler tasks to LSAs and increasing the level of skill of people on the Service Desk so that they can handle a greater percentage of complex incidents. This will also help to build close liaison with second line support.

■ The extra risks to services (and possibly lost benefits) which ensue from allowing developers, third-party staff and business users a greater role (for example, access to ITSM databases) are acceptable.

4.11 Sourcing the suggested roles

Assuming that as many tasks as possible are dealt with outside ITSM (including 'internal outsourcing' to application developers, the business and third parties), Table 4.1 suggests how scaling down might be achieved.

Most tasks shown as candidates for outsourcing could equally well be carried out in-house even in a small organisation. If the organisation happens to contain the skills in-house, then it makes sense to use them. Beware, however, when a member of staff changes that you do not now assume the task needs to be done in-house. An exception is likely to be the specialist occasional tasks, such as capacity planning, which require being up to date on modern innovations and industry direction.

All ITIL functions involve set-up tasks, implementing new procedures, post-implementation review and ongoing monitoring and audit. Establishing these will probably depend on consultancy support, whether or not the function is going to be performed in-house.

Deciding which tasks to keep in-house and which to outsource will depend upon the skills which are available both inside and outside the small IT organisation, not only the skills-set that happens to be in the current staff, but also the availability of consultancy. Special circumstances may also apply, for example, security concerns may dictate that work elements that might otherwise be outsourced should be done in-house.

ITSM processes covered	Approach to the role	Where the role should be
Role 1		
Proactive Problem and Availability Management	Liaise with supporting areas outside ITSM, but maintain responsibility, especially prioritisation	Coordinated within ITSM Mostly done outside ITSM
Role 2		
Incident Management, including second and third line direct support	Maintain process ownership, divest responsibility for action/reporting to business/local administrators/maintainers	Coordinated within ITSM Mostly done outside ITSM
	Or	Or
	Expand role to cover all support services and retain	Within ITSM
Role 3		
Configuration, Change and Release Management	Minimise data collected, devolve authority for change information, treat releases as projects	Divest of collection and assessment
Role 4		
Finance and Resource Capacity Management	Use experts – consultants, third parties or other parts of the organisation	Some internal working but mostly externally delivered
Role 5		
IT Services Continuity Management	External expertise, coordinate with Business Continuity Management	Externally resourced with internal support
Role 6		
Service Level Management, Business and Service Capacity Management, Charging and Relationship Management	Retain and deliver	Internal

Table 4.1   Suggestion of how scaling down might be achieved

5 SOFTWARE TOOLS

Suitable software support tools are essential for IT Service Management to operate effectively. Small IT organisations in particular have to rely on software tools to compensate for their lack of individual specialisms.

Tools for a small IT organisation have substantively the same functionality as tools for larger organisations. This means that smaller organisations have to allocate a larger proportion of their budgets to pay for them. The higher cost can sometimes be balanced against what will probably be lower costs for storing a smaller number of Configuration Items. However, the number of Configuration Item *types* and the relationships between them will not necessarily be less than for a larger organisation. Indeed, within certain types of organisation, for example, scientific establishments, it will be higher, and will require consequentially more set-up and maintenance efforts.

Technology contributes significantly in a number of ways:

- *Integrated Service Management tools* – these will typically cover call logging, incident, problem and change processing, Configuration Management and elements of Service Level Management (SLM). Alternatively these tasks might be addressed by separate software products

- *E-mail* – this can be used for submitting incidents and requests for change (RFCs), and for sending service information to users

- *Intranet/internet* – helping to spread the initial incident recording and resolution workload back to users and local administrators by making information available, for example, through FAQs and through enabling the self-logging of calls by end-users

- *Telephony* – this includes techniques such as automated call distribution (ACD), call queuing, 'intelligent' recorded messages and computer telephony integration (CTI).

5.1 Tools to support Service Support processes

Software to support the greater change function should be an integrated tool with a consistent interface and a repository of common data. Because of the diversity and number of people who can access the data, it is important to have good networking capabilities and access control facilities.

Ideally, the Service Desk/incident logging/Problem Management tool should be based on the same technology as the tool for the greater change function. In particular, it should have a similar user interface, and either share a common database or relate to it through a simple data interchange. And again, because of the need for wide access, the Service Desk tool must be networked and have excellent, flexible access controls.

The above considerations apply to a relatively mature ITSM organisation; however, this is an area where small organisations are not different to larger ones. Even for the smallest organisation, it is no longer possible to deliver effective ITSM processes without adequate software.

The latest integrated Service Management tools are comprehensive, relevant and impressive. They are also expensive, sold aggressively and, for most, certainly designed to apply to a medium-sized to large customer organisation. Processes do need tools support, but to deliver benefits, the tools must be:

- matched to the requirements
- installed and populated appropriately (and this means matched to the specific requirements of the organisation)
- matched to process maturity (for example, no tool, however sophisticated, can support Incident Management if there is an inadequate Incident Management process).

What this means is that a small IT organisation starting from zero will begin to introduce simple improvements and start with immature processes. Tools designed to support mature processes may not be well matched to requirements, but will require serious investment, to both purchase and license, and also in terms of staff resources to administer. Furthermore, as the processes mature, the match between any tool and the processes it supports will decrease, and the tool will need to be restructured or replaced.

So, for a small organisation starting out, it might well be more sensible to begin very simply, for example, by recording calls in a relatively simple database. For an organisation that had no central logging point before, this constitutes a significant step forward at minimal cost. More importantly, it carries minimal overhead and can be thrown away when the organisation is ready to move to the next phase when a more sophisticated solution is justified.

Successful organisations grow and develop, and it is important that small organisations acquire tools that can be scaled according to their needs and process maturity so that the tools grow side by side with the organisation, without the organisation having to invest in new tools.

Another possible cheap alternative that may be available for some small organisations is to obtain tool support through their application service provider, in which case the IT organisation would get access to the tools through web services on the internet site of the external service provider.

Two examples

First

An organisation is 'sold' a sophisticated integrated Service Management product. It rightly claims to support ITIL Service Support + SLM processes. Since there is minimal ITIL knowledge within the organisation, the product is installed 'out of the box'. Support from the supplier is available but charged on a daily basis and, since the tool was expensive, little extra money is available. The product works, but lack of mature processes means only some 10% of the features are used – effectively the product is being used to log and track calls and assign incidents to second and third line support. Some analysis of affected components/user areas is possible, but not well matched to the organisation's current organisational structure and purchasing methods. (Like many companies, the organisational structure evolves rapidly and changes frequently.)

Second

An organisation sets out to introduce a Service Desk to capture calls and information. They take on a computer science student for the summer vacation and use them to develop a simple Access database to record basic details on the calls they take and how they react to them. The first version has some troubles, but the student reworks it and they are able to record all calls and log them, know where the call has been assigned and track progress through to second and third line support. Some analysis is possible, but it is hard to match it to the current structure of the organisation.

In these two scenarios, both organisations have the same amount of management information from their support tools, but one has spent more money and is locked into a route whereas the other can now look at the situation afresh with the knowledge they have learned through hands-on experience and specify what they need a tool to do for the next stage of their ITIL maturity programme.

5.2   Tools to support Service Delivery processes

The Service Delivery processes do not flow together in the same way that the Service Support ones do and this is reflected in the more fragmented nature of tool support.

Some of the more direct measures relating to SLM will be obtained from the Service Support data. However, this will comprise performance against times to respond to calls, restore service etc., and will not cover all the data and measures SLM requires.

Requirements for Availability Management tools can often be put together from the detailed data kept by the Service Support tools, with a further requirement for a simple predictive modelling component via a link to a spreadsheet.

As most aspects of Capacity Management, costing and contingency planning are probably going to be outsourced, tools which do more than collect data about the system's performance and usage may not be needed in-house. If these functions are retained in-house, the specialists involved will know what software support is appropriate, and will probably be able to supply and use what is required.

5.2.1   Knowledge base

While a small organisation will be able to afford neither sophisticated knowledge-based software, nor the major administrative overheads that larger organisations might manage, there is still much benefit from recording learned information in a reusable fashion, for example, through the organisation's intranet or e-mail, or through public folders on the network.

Key and relatively easy to implement features are possible, such as:

- consistent methods of capturing incident data – essential for matching similar incidents should they recur
- accessible repository of diagnostic scripts for Service Desk staff use
- repository of known errors and workaround information
- repository of documented RFCs and Service Level Agreement (SLA) information.

Even in a small organisation, the knowledge base will benefit from the inclusion of Forward Schedule of Change, projected service availability etc. The repository will include problems, as well as known errors, and can also contain FAQs and Hints & Tips.

5.3   Implementation of software tools[1]

Using software tools successfully is not just a question of buying them and loading them on to a hardware platform. Even in the smallest of organisations, introducing a software tool must be treated as a project which establishes the need for the tool, justifies its acquisition and makes sure that the right resources are put into installing it. The need for a controlled justification and implementation is not dependent on the size or scale of either the software or the organisation. The project's purpose is to implement changes to the processes, not just revised software. This means that even a simple database installation needs to be carefully implemented, taking the views of *all* areas of the business that might be affected.

---

1   This section is based on ideas presentations by Dorothy Graham, Grove Consultants 1991–1994.

The informal nature of small IT organisations makes it tempting to think that Service Management tools can be implemented quickly at minimal cost. This is simply not true. There are some established maxims for introducing tools which apply to all kinds of support tools in all sizes of IT organisation.

- The cost of the tool is more than its purchase price. Costs to consider after the initial investment include:
  - preparing data for initial upload
  - staff training and familiarisation– in addition to basic training, staff will need practice before they are competent
  - developing and implementing any revised processes that the tool either requires or permits

- Free to use shareware with no support may turn out more expensive over time than commercial software with good support included

- Introducing a new function will not save money; a new, comprehensive Service Management tool will make new processes and new information possible. This may improve services to customers. However, in the short term at least, introducing new functions will need extra time and money

- Automated chaos is just faster chaos. Before installing a tool, it is always worth spending time to try to improve current practices. For example, if configuration inventory figures are inaccurate, a state-of-the-art Configuration Management database will just provide a very detailed record of items that don't exist.

5.3.1 'Silver bullet' lifecycle

No tool is a silver bullet, solving every problem at a stroke: it will take time before savings and improvements start to show.

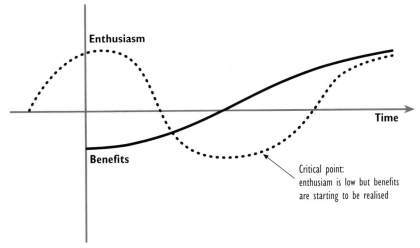

Figure 5.1 Enthusiasm for a software tool may be at its lowest point just as the benefits are being realised

This can affect people's enthusiasm for the new tool. Initially they are keen but when learning difficulties and teething troubles appear, this enthusiasm will wane. At this point, there is a real danger of disillusionment killing off the tool, committing the organisation to a new round of problems and eventual disillusionment the next time. Management have a key role to play at this point, encouraging staff to persevere to the stage where, with familiarity, the tool becomes easy to use and starts to produce the benefits that were promised.

Example

A small IT organisation installed a Service Support tool without realising the amount of staff time that would be needed, and the degree of management involvement for making decisions. Consequently the installation was rushed, and wrong decisions or, even worse, no decisions were taken at crucial moments. The result was a tool that did not support Incident and Problem Management. Links to the data were inadequate and the base data was suspect and out of date. People working on the Service Desk felt cheated and unhappy. When last heard from, the organisation was replacing the tool in question with a new one. But no plans had been made to make extra resources available for taking it on and making it work.

And so the cycle repeats itself. At least this time the Service Desk staff did not expect so much . . .

Also under this heading comes the warning not to believe everything the sales staff promise. If the organisation's level of technical knowledge is a problem, a third party should be brought in, either from elsewhere in the organisation, from a consultancy or from another organisation that already has the tool or a different one. This is crucial advice for a small organisation, which is unlikely to have the specialist negotiating expertise that a large organisation might have in a procurement situation.

5.3.2   Justifying tools

The smaller the organisation, the higher the percentage of the budget a support tool is likely to be. This makes it harder for small organisations to justify tools, and especially to justify an integrated Service Management tool rather than one which only does a part of the job. Nevertheless, even the smallest of organisations will probably still benefit from using an integrated Service Support tool, because:

- By combining many functions in a single tool, the tool should provide:
    - a cheaper option in the long run than several different tools
    - a single learning curve, allowing savings to accrue more quickly

- an integrated picture of incidents and errors, allowing Service Desk staff to resolve more incidents without escalation
- an economy of scale by using the tools for extended functions outside just IT services
- greater data integrity, since data is held once and shared by all users

■ The procedures established will minimise dependence on one or two individuals

■ Holding information electronically rather than on paper is much safer and cheaper, with important implications for contingency and back-up. Copying an electronic database many times is trivial; copying a paper data bank is almost impossible.

5.4   User guides

If user guides are simple to follow, a well-presented and up-to-date handbook can greatly ease the day-to-day burden falling upon small ITSM sections. Details on the suggested contents of such a user handbook are set out in Annex B. At their best, these documents can:

■ Reduce the number of trivial incidents caused by users not understanding their systems and reporting as incidents simple things they could fix themselves, such as switching equipment on, resetting systems or even waiting long enough for things to happen

■ Encourage people to use services more widely by explaining what they are, what they can and can't do and how to access them

■ Encourage people to follow procedures, especially RFCs, by laying them out clearly and either providing appropriate forms or describing the electronic logging process

■ Provide a single point for all the IT information needed at users' workstations, including information for third-party repairers such as settings and options for equipment.

But if documents are difficult to understand, incomplete, wrong or out of date (as they unfortunately are in many organisations) they merely compound the problems they are designed to solve. Additionally, these documents need to be easy to find. If a user has to look too hard for the information needed to get help on their own, they will not follow through with that effort but will instead fall back to calling the Service Desk.

To make sure documents provide real and valuable benefits, it is worth following some simple rules:

■ *Ensure someone is responsible for the accuracy of the documentation* – this should be a high priority role for SLM and/or the Service Desk. The change control process must include changes to the handbook as part of any change to IT services

■ *Allocate resources to maintain documentation properly* – if money and resources are not budgeted for, all the time, effort and money spent on developing the guide in the first place will be wasted. Consider hiring a professional writer to simplify the language and make it more accessible to people not as technically sophisticated. Alternatively, these skills may be available within the organisation, perhaps in customer areas which would reap the benefits of investing support to IT

■ *Involve users in creating and maintaining the documentation* – business sections can include help and advice on the procedures specific to their work and/or location

■ *Test the documents* – testing should be both from an IT point of view, for technical accuracy, and from the users' perspective, for accuracy in the work context and usability

■ *Publicise the documentation to customers* – customers should know what is in the documentation and how to use it. It must look and sound easy to use. One approach is to use friendly names to help keep guides in users' minds. Real life examples include:

- HINTS *Handbook for INformation Technology*
- LITES *Local IT Equipment and Services manual*

■ *Make sure ITSM staff are familiar with it* – they are then likely to refer users to it for guidance

■ *Control copies* – check that those who should retain an up-to-date copy do in fact have one. Possibly the Configuration Management or asset control system could be used to record this. Audits should check that it is:

- where it is expected to be (if not, it is worth checking the reason – perhaps it has been moved to somewhere more useful)
- up to date
- well used, thumbed and ragged (if not, the number and type of incidents logged from that location should be checked).

For an electronic handbook, it is also important to realise that:

■ many users will print it out, preferring to read paper rather than screens, so it is easy for users to be referring to out-of-date documents

■ if the system goes down, so does the handbook!

6 PROCESSES ON THE FRINGE OF ITSM

Within a large IT organisation, there will be several independent divisions. As the picture is scaled down, fewer people mean that the number of divisions will also reduce.

Tasks which are independent in a larger organisation must fit into whatever divisions the small organisation provides. Tasks which generally provide a service to customers are best placed under the ITSM umbrella.

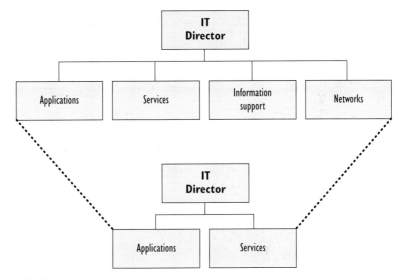

Figure 6.1 The shrinking organisation

6.1 System security

IT managers are responsible for safeguarding customers' data while that data is within their domain. Since virtually all IT environments are subject to one or more threats to data, equipment or facilities, this is an important responsibility, and managers must use their limited resources to provide the most appropriate protection possible. In addition, if data is subject to data protection legislation, there is a requirement to make every effort to protect all personnel data. This means putting in place appropriate IT, procedural and physical security controls.

6.1.1 Security Risk Analysis

Security Risk Analysis provides a way of identifying threats, vulnerabilities and risks to systems, staff and facilities. Each risk is assessed, often in terms of historical or actuarial data, so that its impact can be costed. Then a range of measures to counter the threats can be planned and costed, and cost-benefit recommendations drawn up. Depending on the budget available and the level of risk that is acceptable, a selection of measures can be introduced.

Unless there are experienced security staff in the organisation, the initial security assessment should be done by an external consultant with a proven track record in this field. Tools such as CRAMM (CCTA Risk Assessment and Management Method) capture many years of security best practice to help professionals with such assessments, but they will not entirely replace human expertise. Using untrained staff is counter-productive, lulling the IT manager into a false sense of security.

6.1.2   Detecting viruses

Although organisations are understandably reluctant to 'go public', the available evidence, reinforced by considerable anecdotal and informal research, indicates that viruses and similar malicious software pose a major threat to business viability.

In our 'global electronic community' every organisation is susceptible to this kind of threat and should take an appropriate degree of protection. Appropriate defence techniques include:

- *Installing virus detection and firewall software* – this has now become all but universal, but obtaining the software needs to be accompanied by processes to ensure it is installed on all appropriate PCs and servers, and that both the software and associated data files are updated appropriately

- *Screening all incoming media* – loading any suspect software initially on to a stand-alone machine dedicated to virus detection

- *Raising awareness* – this means constantly reinforcing staff and users' awareness of both the risks and the virus protection measures in place. Most importantly, staff should be kept aware of the signs of virus infection and the action to take if they suspect an infection on their PC, for example, immediately disconnect the network connection and call the Service Desk

- *Holding master software in quarantine* – implementing a Definitive Software Library ensures it cannot become infected.

6.1.3   Perception of virus-checking facilities

In support of the organisation's virus detection policy ITSM must offer a service that is fast, easy and user-friendly.

If it is perceived as not being all of these, it will not be used, representing the worst of all worlds since you will have all the disadvantages of a virus protection system with no benefits. That is, you will have:

- the expense of virus protection
- performance constraints on the system
- administrative and training overheads for staff

but still have

- inadequate protection.

It is worth considering *anything* which might make virus screening easier and so more widely used. Draconian threats and punishments for those who bypass the protection do not work – they merely provide a scapegoat if things go wrong, which is no help at all to a business crippled by loss of data or operational facilities. Ways of improving cooperation might include:

- a no-blame policy to encourage staff to raise the alarm at the earliest sign of a possible infection
- making sure that any games software is authorised as virus free – many organisations ban all games to prevent viruses, but others find this merely encourages their illicit introduction
- checking how effective protection is, possibly by:
  - seeding benign viruses
  - holding software audits
  - carrying out anonymous surveys.

The user-friendliness of the service ITSM provides will depend upon many factors including:

- the perceived risk of infection
- the amount of predicted damage caused by infection
- the independence of users
- the common sense of users – there is no reliable link between users' common sense and their intelligence, IT awareness or grade.

6.2 Business Continuity Management

Business Continuity Management (BCM) is about making sure that organisations can continue to operate after a disaster. BCM involves:

- identifying the business processes which need protection
- identifying cost-effective ways of reducing risks to the processes
- identifying key support functions for each process
- working out how to provide that support in any foreseeable disaster scenario.

IT Service Continuity Management (ITSCM) planning is concerned with how to deliver an appropriate level of IT support for the business in the event of a disaster. The ITIL chapter on ITSCM describes in detail the various options for ensuring continuity.

But while it is essential to preserve IT services if a business is to survive a disaster, it is not enough. There are many examples of organisations failing to survive in spite of a heavy investment in IT contingency, simply because they ignored other much more modest precautions to ensure business continuity. Especially in a small organisation, the IT organisation can take the lead on business continuity, since their own plans are likely to be more developed than those of any other operational or support area.

On more than one occasion the IT services manager has been responsible for triggering the introduction of BCM within an organisation.

> A good example is the submission of an ITSM contingency plan to the managing director. The plan was accompanied by a note from the IT services manager.
>
> This note explained that she understood the commercial significance of the organisation's disaster recovery plans, and the need for confidentiality. She realised this was why she did not have access to them. It was essential though that the ITSM plans fitted in with the organisation's plans as a whole. Could the managing director (who would of course be privy to the full disaster recovery plans) therefore confirm that the ITSM contingency plans as submitted were consistent with those of the whole company?
>
> Within a week the IT services manager was responsible for managing a feasibility study on BCM for the organisation.

6.3 Data management

ITSM is likely to be closely involved with many aspects of data management. This involvement includes:

- *acting as data steward* – this means being responsible for administrating and promoting changes to data schema and definitions
- *providing administration for databases* – ITSM can be responsible for the day-to-day administration of any database management systems (DBMS).

Regarding data as part of the IT infrastructure, and therefore as part of ITSM's responsibility, has many advantages. These include:

- improved change impact analysis
- improved Capacity Management
- more attention given to data availability and contingency issues
- seeing data as a corporate resource.

Dangers inherent in including data management in ITSM's responsibilities include:

- underestimating the strategic importance of data management
- over-dependence on the DBMS software.

6.4 Software maintenance

In all IT organisations, strong links exist between Problem Management and software maintenance. In a small organisation, software maintenance is likely to be a part-time or even an ad hoc role for systems developers. The organisation may choose to place the entire responsibility for managing software incidents with the application development staff, with the Service Desk responsibility restricted to logging requests and passing them on.

6.5 Testing and acceptance of hardware and software

Adequate testing is vital if there is to be a good perception of the IT services. In too many cases, organisations feel that their ITSM processes are failing them because of large numbers of incidents and long delays in their resolution, when in fact many of these incidents are due to errors that should have been detected before the service or change went into live use.

Experience shows that money saved by reducing the quality of a change or new service (for example, by inadequate testing) requires several times as much money to be spent further down the line in detecting and resolving incidents, and the lost business time caused by system outages.

Small IT organisations are not likely to develop specialist independent testing sections. Testing of applications which have been developed in-house can be done by cross-team testing within the development section. Types of testing that ITSM might usefully be involved with include:

- *operational testing* – this is appropriate since ITSM will operate the systems when they are part of the live service
- *load and capacity testing* – this ensures that there is enough capacity available to support the new or revised service

■ *acceptance testing of hardware* – this should be done before hardware is connected to the live service

■ *installation testing, fall–back testing, integration testing* and others.

In a small IT organisation, ITSM is in a particularly good position to ensure that all the components of an IT service operate together and to work with users on the acceptance testing of a system.

It is possible to outsource such testing, but organisations will have to balance the advantages of this against the awareness that their own staff and customers will be using the system for years to come. If the staff and customers are involved in acceptance testing, they are likely to be happy and supportive of the system when it goes live.

6.5.1   Business testing

However carefully the component parts of a business process have been tested, what really matters is how well everything works together. This has given rise to the belief that the only real test is live running – that the proof of the pudding is in the eating. But while ultimately this must be true, it is often possible to test the whole process before live running. This kind of business testing is likely to be a more cost-effective and practical proposition in a small organisation, with simpler logistics and more cooperative staff.

Example

A professional sports team offers supporters season tickets for their games. These are applied for on a range of different forms (from the club newsletter, on fliers, downloadable from club website etc.) designed to be read by a scanner in conjunction with optical character recognition (OCR) software. All the technical components of the equipment are procured and tested, and work above expectations.

However, when the system is introduced, it does not deliver the business service required due to a combination of issues such as:

■ preparing the forms – removing them from the envelope, stacking in correct alignment

■ sorting and collating the different types of form

■ issues with forms that have been folded behaving differently to the flat forms used for system testing

■ OCR software not matching expected performance when faced with fans' handwriting compared to test material.

The first time the full business service was tried was for live running – no attempts had been made to simulate and test it, only the individual pieces.

6.6 Spreadsheets, databases and other user software tools

All too often spreadsheets and local databases are created by end-users and subjected to little if any testing. They are not seen as software development and so don't follow the same rules as any other development. People seem to have total faith in figures that are produced by the computer, especially if they are presented in the sophisticated formats available from modern software products, even if they have not been tested or verified. Because of this, many important business decisions are now made from information in user-developed spreadsheets and databases, without any assurance that the figures are accurately captured and calculated. Small organisations seem particularly susceptible to this since financial and business planning is often done on simpler software rather than specialist (and commercially trialled and tested) software such as SAP. Susceptibility is also increased since the software is more likely to be used by higher-level staff within an organisation, who typically feel less constrained by rules and internal procedural requirements.

So, small organisations should address the situation in so far as they can. Some simple techniques might include:

- *Providing training in testing spreadsheets* – it might even be possible to restrict access to those who have been trained

- *Raising awareness by telling horror stories* – senior managers can be told horror stories from their own organisation about spreadsheets which weren't tested properly. If there are no horror stories, this is probably because either nobody uses spreadsheets or the errors haven't been spotted yet

- *Explaining the pitfalls of self-testing* – there are good psychological reasons why it is impossible for writers of spreadsheets or databases (or indeed a piece of prose) to self-test and find their own errors

- *Providing a testing service* – the IT organisation tests user-developed spreadsheets itself, on the basis that this costs the organisation less than allowing the mistakes to 'come out in the wash'.

ITSM staff themselves are likely to want to develop spreadsheets and databases for management information. They should not be too proud to take advice from application developers and testers in the IT organisation. And they should remember that an external test is always worthwhile.

7 MEASURING PERFORMANCE

An IT organisation's performance is judged by the quality of the service it provides to users, and on how well it can fulfil service level requirements.

A good level of performance depends not only on the ability of IT systems to support the user workload, but also on the efficiency of the ITSM team in making the most of them. Organisations should constantly think about how to improve their performance, questioning the professionalism of their interface with users, the effectiveness of their Problem Management system, their ability to manage risk and so on.

7.1 Objectives and metrics

In order to improve performance, there must be some measure of what that performance is, against which improvements or otherwise can be judged. There are many measurable items in ITSM; it makes sense for an organisation to:

- identify those items which matter most to their situation
- measure the current performance
- set objectives for improvement
- monitor measures to see if objectives have been met.

The prime rule is to identify and then measure what is important to the business, not be sidetracked into measuring what is easy for IT to measure in the hope it might turn out to be useful. If a few key metrics are identified correctly, monitoring can give management a good ongoing indication of the organisation's performance in terms of delivering a quality IT service efficiently and effectively. However, as with all things, it costs time and money to produce and interpret measures. So as well as monitoring the metrics in terms of the organisation's performance, it is important to monitor their relevance as measures. For a small organisation, where the overheads of measurement can quickly become significant, it is worthwhile reducing the number of variables measured by identifying:

- *measures that vary together* – if different measures are not independent, it is probably only worth measuring one of them
- *expensive measures* – some measures are much more expensive to monitor than others
- *ambiguous measures* – these can be influenced by a number of different factors and are open to multiple interpretations
- *widely fluctuating measures* – except where they can be identified with obvious corresponding peaks and troughs.

Broadly speaking, there are two kinds of measures:

- *external* – these directly measure the scale or quality of the delivered service
- *internal* – these measure the internal processes underpinning the service.

Some measures can straddle this boundary and give indications of performance both above and below the waterline, such as the number of calls to the Service Desk.

Case example

The number of calls to the Service Desk is one of the most popular measures to monitor, and yet one of the hardest to interpret. It is a very popular measure, primarily because it is very easy to collect. But it is very hard to interpret – nobody calls the Service Desk because they want to, but because they need to. Thus the measurement depends on other variables.

Possible reasons for an increase in calls can be manifold and contradictory. For example:

- a bad Service Desk might attract more calls because users have to keep calling until their incident is resolved
- a good Service Desk might receive more calls because users, encouraged by a good service, are using it more often
- a new release or change of software will attract more calls
- any change of staff or working practices will result in more calls because users are not so familiar with the service
- the work may be seasonal, so that less familiar parts of the IT system are being used at certain times of the year
- there may be something wrong with the delivery of the service, such as:
  - changes not being properly tested
  - software getting out of step across a distributed system
  - network or hardware going down.

All this shows that metrics are not independent and are not easy to interpret; just because something is easy to count does not mean that it should become a key ITSM measurement.

7.1.1   External metrics

Measurements which directly affect customers' ability to use the IT service will appear within Service Level Agreements (SLAs). Most small organisations would find it worthwhile to measure:

- availability of IT at the desktop

- time between reporting an incident and being told it is resolved
- time the Service Desk takes to:
    - respond to a caller and log an incident
    - resolve an incident (broken down by category and priority)
- time taken to process change requests, including:
    - acknowledging a request for change (RFC)
    - approving or rejecting an RFC
    - implementing approved changes, including the success rate.

These external measures relate directly to the service being delivered to the customer above the waterline (see Figure 2.3).

There will also need to be measurements of the actual workload that fulfilling the SLAs implies – this is probably kept to an agreed limit in the SLAs.

7.1.2   Internal metrics

In order to deliver the required levels of service, there will be many underpinning, internal ITSM processes which ITSM must measure and monitor to maintain its services. These metrics will not be directly relevant to the customer. They might include:

- availability of components, such as:
    - networks
    - servers
    - software packages
    - communication and systems software
    - electricity
- breakdown of the time taken to fully repair each component, including:
    - recognising and recording the fault
    - maintainers' response
    - actually fixing components
    - restoring the system
    - informing customers
- Service Desk statistics, consisting of:
    - number of incidents solved at first level and number requiring escalation
    - time spent on each call
- contribution to the change process, measured by:
    - comments on RFCs from staff members
    - length and frequency of change meetings
    - number of changes requiring back-out and resubmission
    - errors found during testing and stages where they were discovered.

7.1.3 Measuring customer perceptions

All the measures described so far are 'hard' – that is, they can be expressed as numbers. It is the way those numbers change over time, taken with the changes in workload and other external influences, that matter to ITSM managers. But IT organisations should not forget that hard measures are not, by any means, the whole picture.

As American management guru Tom Peters observed:

> *Perception is all there is . . . The man who said you can only manage what you can measure was probably a very good scientist – he certainly never ran a successful business.*

The typical IT professional has a mind-set which lends itself to absolute numeric measures of performance, so they expect to be judged in that manner. But the majority of business users are unlikely to think in the same way. They will be more interested in how the service feels. For example, one of the most quoted statistics for Service Desks is the number of times the telephone is not answered within four rings. This statistic has the attraction of being easy to collect. In practice, what affects the customer's perception of the Service Desk is the first ten seconds of conversation after the telephone is answered. The right words and attitudes can produce instant forgiveness for that fifth ring. However, this is not at all easy to measure.

Research on customer satisfaction and expectations in the airline industry shows that customer perceptions are principally affected by a few key moments of interaction with staff. These are fairly easy to spot for airlines – at the check-in desk, or boarding the plane. Applying this to the ITSM environment shows how vital the first few seconds of conversation between customer and Service Desk are.

Customers will judge a service by how much use it is to them in their work. They will be willing to forgive a surprising number of troubles and inadequacies if they perceive that IT systems and support services, for them, add value to their work.

IT organisations should try always to establish what goes right, as well as where they fail to meet targets. Often this kind of added value goes unnoticed. It is the service above and beyond the call of duty that really impresses users; but it can be eclipsed and prevented by a culture too concerned with mundane everyday measures.

Conventional techniques such as customer satisfaction surveys are well suited to small establishments, since a wide coverage of the customer base can be achieved. In very small environments, results will be excessively affected by familiarity and social contact between customer and IT, and may be disproportionately affected by a few dissatisfied customers.

As well as formal surveying and perception gathering, the view from the Service Desk in a small organisation will be more representative than in a large one – where one or two Service Desk staff will see a broad enough range of calls to form an accurate picture of what the customer base feels about the IT service.

The relatively small customer base, and faster and shorter communication chains also make it feasible to use facilitated workshops to discuss customer satisfaction and how to improve it. As is the case for any exercise in gathering customer views, unless action is taken on those views and requests, credibility and reputation will be damaged rather than enhanced, and customers will be left feeling they wasted their time by contributing when their requests have been ignored.

7.2 Health checks and assessments

It is always difficult for any organisation to really know how well it is doing its job. For small organisations, comparisons and measures of performance are especially hard since there is considerable diversity between organisations, and service providers will be adapted to the idiosyncrasies of their organisation. Also smaller organisations are unlikely to be able to access internal resources who can be objective in observing processes and procedures – larger organisations can often bring in someone who knows the overall company and policy, but not the specific division being observed.

7.2.1 Assessment of processes

However, with the constant need to justify expenditure and to examine alternative sourcing options, an evaluation is often useful and expected. In order to help that evaluation process, there are several methods and techniques available, including assessment methods, health check packages and structured questionnaires. Typical approaches include:

- *Self-assessments* – structured approaches are available including:
  - OGC/*it*SMF self-assessment questionnaires for each core ITIL process help an organisation to compare their approach with the guidance set out in each chapter of the *Service Support* and *Service Delivery* books – downloadable for free from www.itsmf.com
  - BS15000 self-assessment workbook – essentially the elements of BS15000, the standard for IT Service Management, expressed as questions, allowing an organisation to identify whether they carry out the requirements of the standard – available as a hard copy or electronic product from BSI (www.bsi-global.com) or *it*SMF (www.itsmf.com)
- *Externally delivered assessments* – many specialist and general consultancy suppliers will deliver an assessment or health check for an organisation. The type of assessment (for example, whether it is numerically expressed against guidance requirements or more intuitive suggestions based on experience) can vary enormously. Small organisations may feel it is important that the approach can be tailored to their specific goals rather than just delivering a report comparing them against generic guidance.

In either case, the assessment itself should be seen as a tool for improvement, not an end in itself, and therefore the exercise should deliver two elements:

- an assessment of current performance
- a plan for improvement.

7.2.2 Plan for improvement

This details specific target areas for improvement and, ideally, measurable objectives. It is of far greater use to the working IT organisation than an assessment report on conformance to best practice guidance because it shows how to concentrate limited resources in areas that will increase effectiveness and efficiency.

The quality of the improvement proposals depends on:

- management commitment to the exercise and business priorities
- staff attitudes
- the skills of the individuals carrying out the exercise (the method used will help pinpoint the weak areas, but is unlikely to offer solutions tailored to your environment).

7.2.3 Implementing health checks

The consultant performing the health check must be familiar with best business practice in the areas being checked. However refined the method or questionnaire, this kind of exercise is, at most, 50% science, with the rest being more of an art, depending on knowledge, experience, skill in data gathering and the ability to gain cooperation from staff who may initially be hostile and suspicious.

The effort involved in performance of a health check will vary depending upon the scope of the check and the size of the organisation. In general, however, a health check should be an initial investigation, not a detailed study. Funds and resources are almost always scarce in small organisations, and if considerable effort is being proposed, consider the following questions:

- *Are any benefits identified likely to be outweighed by the cost of the check itself?*
- *Can you cope with all the information and proposals that will be generated from this work?* You will have limited resources, funds and time to take the improvement plans on board, especially management time to champion them
- *Is the proposal too wide-ranging?* Perhaps it would be better to spend less at the start to identify which areas would benefit from a more detailed look
- *What else could the money be spent on?* Running the organisation comes first, improving it second.

Small organisations are more likely than large ones to benefit from a more general view, where health checks of more limited scope are sensible. So it is much harder in the small organisation to make sure the right survey is being carried out. Many of the methods in current favour are aimed at particular parts of the IT organisation, for example, software production, ITSM or security. All of these areas and methods have overlap. For a wide-ranging view, the outside consultancy has to have expertise across the whole range of IT disciplines; ideally it can provide individuals experienced and qualified in assessments and health checks over more than one area. It could be sensible to spend one or two days of consultancy on a high-level exercise which would explain the options, provide evidence and justify any accurately targeted further spend.

7.3   Where to go for advice

Staff in small IT organisations often feel isolated; compared to larger organisations, they have fewer fellow IT professionals within their daily environment. (The benefit, of course, is that they are more likely to be in daily professional and social contact with non-IT staff helping to develop a wider and more balanced view of their role within the organisation.) There are sources of advice and comparison available. Some potential contacts are given here:

IT Service Management Forum (*it*SMF) – The *it*SMF is an independent, not-for-profit organisation dedicated to the development and promotion of best practice in ITSM. It is wholly owned and principally run by its members. There are chapters in more than 30 countries, and an international coordinating body. All of the national chapters provide a mechanism for local members to meet and discuss mutual concerns and ideas. Many chapters either have or are considering specialist groups for small organisations. Information is available through the website www.itsmf.com

Other IT organisations – your problems are rarely unique. Similar IT organisations are likely to have encountered similar problems to yourself. Consult with more than one such organisation. Identify elements of the approaches best suited to your own environment. Formulate an approach and discuss with these organisations. *it*SMF can often make connections and contacts, as can industry user groups (where an IT sub-group may be operating or worth initiating) and local business associations.

Consultancy – consider the use of external consultants. Once again, solicit recommendations from managers of other IT organisations.

Regulatory bodies – information concerning specialist areas can often be obtained from government or other regulatory organisations.

Annex A IT SERVICE MANAGEMENT – TASK ALLOCATION GUIDE

A.1 Introduction

Section 4.10 discusses the options available to an IT organisation for meeting ITSM task requirements. Five options were identified and explained briefly. This annex repeats and expands those options, and then offers a breakdown of the ITSM tasks, indicating the possible sourcing of each task against the five identified options. This annex is written on the assumption that a decision has been made to retain an in-house IT services function.

A.1.2 Breakdown of possible sourcing of ITSM functions

The five categories identified and used throughout this annex are as follows.

ITSM provides

These tasks need to be retained and performed by an in-house IT services section. They fall into two broad categories:

- roles that interface directly with the customer and user, such as the day-to-day Service Desk and user communications, negotiating and agreeing service levels and initial consideration of change requests

- monitoring and controlling the underpinning ITSM functions.

ITSM jointly provides

These tasks can be performed by IT services in partnership with another provider (this may be third party or in-house application development or business organisations). The identity of the suggested partner(s) can be found in the grid below. Much of any necessary initiation work will be a partnership between external consultants and in-house staff.

Business provides

These tasks are best supplied by staff within the business function (although the cost may still be seen as part of supporting IT within the organisation). This approach is recommended for tasks such as:

- defining the aims of the ITSM function

- IT service (and business) continuity for equipment and services under the day-to-day control of users

- local filtering of incidents and day-to-day operation of locally sited equipment (local systems administrators).

Third party provides

These tasks are best outsourced to external experts/service providers and mostly require specialist knowledge and skills. Such skills are required for only a small percentage of the time and it is thus not economically viable to recruit and/or train in-house staff with those skills. Indeed the range of such knowledge across the ITSM functions would make it impossible to provide all these tasks using in-house staff in anything less than a medium-sized IT organisation.

The other major area of third-party input is in the establishment of new or changed procedures and requirements. This type of work is especially suited to third-party supply since:

- by its very nature it is additional work, over and above the current tasks of supporting customers, and thus the introduction of additional resources to meet it is logical[1]

- it is an area where previous experience is beneficial; again, this experience must come from outside the organisation, either from a third party or new staff

- an external view may be more objective and less influenced by current and historical practice.

Developer provides

These tasks are supplied by the application development and/or maintenance staff, covering functions that:

- require applications expertise and experience, such as enhancing, modifying and testing software support tools

- define and establish ITSM parameters within new and changed applications, such as capacity and availability requirements

- manage problems and errors, especially in correcting software faults or preventing software-related incidents.

A.2   Caveats

This annex has been developed against a general concept of a small IT organisation's ITSM needs; it cannot be prescriptive nor apply to all possible circumstances. In

---

1   However, many organisations find it sensible to bring in external resource to deliver the day job, making the in-house resource free to contribute to process review exercises, bringing much-needed local knowledge and experience to the exercise, possibly in collaboration with external consultants.

particular the picture will be modified (heavily in some instances) by the following influences:

- the particular skills and experience that happen to be available from the staff currently working in:
    - IT services
    - application development
    - business communities
- consultancy services available (either independent or perhaps within a parent organisation's IT staff)
- financial constraints – it costs money to hire consultants, recruit new staff, retrain existing staff or do new things, and the need to balance requirements and funds is one well known and understood by managers everywhere
- existing strengths and weaknesses in the current ITSM offering
- perceived needs of the customer base.

A.3 Task-by-task breakdown of possible sourcing for ITSM

The following tables indicate suggested sourcing for:

- generic tasks – those needed to introduce the ITIL approach and those concerned with planning, implementing, monitoring and controlling that are common to all (or many) of the individual functions
- tasks specific to the individual 'core' ITIL functions (i.e. those within Service Support and Service Delivery.

It is important to recognise that retaining a task in-house does not mean that other parties will not be involved via consultation and normal customer/supplier relations. Conversely, the 'offloading' of a task outside ITSM does not absolve ITSM of appropriate involvement, but indicates that control and responsibility for the execution of the tasks has been passed over.

A.3.1 Generic ITSM tasks

	ITSM provides	ITSM jointly provides	Business provides	Third party provides	Developer provides
Tasks in role definition					
defining the mission statement for the IT service		✓	✓	✓	
setting aims and objectives for the IT service		✓	✓	✓	
Tasks in awareness raising					
communicating the benefits of the IT service	✓			✓	
circulating information through seminars, meetings, leaflets or circulars	✓			✓	
Tasks in planning					
producing a statement of requirements for the specified ITIL functions	✓			✓	
defining detailed requirements				✓	
quantifying the workload of the new service	✓			✓	
producing guidelines about how the service will work — its structure and relationship to the organisational structure	✓			✓	
specifying target performance measurements	✓		✓	✓	
designing the process the function is to perform, including support for it	✓			✓	
producing an implementation plan	✓			✓	
defining ITSM staff training requirements	✓			✓	
describing benefits, costs and possible problems	✓		✓	✓	

	ITSM provides	ITSM jointly provides	Business provides	Third party provides	Developer provides
Tasks in implementation					
developing and validating the process	✓			✓	
installing software and equipment	✓			✓	
customising packaged computer tools				✓	✓
testing the process	✓		✓		✓
creating inventories for software and equipment	✓			✓	
writing support documents	✓			✓	
training staff	✓			✓	
carrying out acceptance training	✓		✓		
going live	✓				
Tasks in post-implementation review and audit					
reconciling requirements with reality — checking that services are providing what users want		✓		✓	
comparing actual activity levels with forecasts		✓		✓	
assessing how staff feel about the service		✓		✓	
reviewing effectiveness and efficiency		✓		✓	
identifying benefits			✓	✓	
reviewing the management of the project		✓		✓	
preparing review reports		✓		✓	
carrying out regular audits				✓	
monitoring, reviewing and fine-tuning how effective the service is	✓				

	ITSM provides	ITSM jointly provides	Business provides	Third party provides	Developer provides
Tasks in supporting the development cycle					
making sure that requirements for running and maintaining systems are taken into account from the start					✓
creating testing strategies for IT services	✓				✓
assessing the impact of new or changed systems on the existing IT infrastructure and services	✓				
understanding from the start what everyone will need from the system	✓				✓
Tasks in achieving customer focus					
advising and helping IT customers to make the best use of IT services		✓	✓		
passing on customers' views and ensuring comments are acted on		✓	✓		
following up customers' complaints	✓				
monitoring how customers perceive the quality of their IT services		✓	✓		
encouraging internal user groups			✓		
initiating customer care programmes	✓				
making sure that properly trained Service Desk staff are available	✓				
providing feedback to staff		✓	✓		
tracking the customers' business needs to ensure IT services continue to meet them		✓	✓		

A.3.2   Incident Management

	ITSM provides	ITSM jointly provides	Business provides	Third party provides	Developer provides
Tasks in incident control					
providing second level support (after Service Desk) for diagnosing and resolving difficult or major incidents				✓	✓
acting as coordinator for other specialist support (possibly via the Service Desk)	✓				
Service Desk day-to-day tasks					
providing a customer interface	✓		✓		
managing the incident control system	✓				
acting as support for business operations			✓	✓	✓
providing management information	✓				
providing information to users (bulletins etc.)		✓		✓	
Tasks in setting up a Service Desk					
assessing the volume of calls you'll need to process	✓		✓		
deciding on a centralised or distributed structure				✓	
investigating what type of call logging to use (the hardware, the software and the telephone system)				✓	
defining the procedures for customers to follow when calling the Service Desk		✓	✓	✓	
laying down the procedures for Service Desk staff in dealing with enquiries	✓				
training for customers and Service Desk staff		✓		✓	
deciding on use of scripts		✓		✓	

A.3.3 Problem Management

	ITSM provides	ITSM jointly provides	Business provides	Third party provides	Developer provides
Tasks in problem control					
identifying, diagnosing and recording the root causes of incidents		✓		✓	✓
carrying out severity analysis and providing appropriate support	✓			✓	✓
identifying potential problems before they can cause disruption to IT services	✓			✓	✓
maintaining problems database		✓		✓	✓
Tasks in error control					
initiating requests for change (RFCs), to prevent incidents from occurring	✓				
putting right known errors, under the control of Change Management		✓		✓	✓
maintaining known errors database		✓		✓	✓

A.3.4 Change Management

	ITSM provides	ITSM jointly provides	Business provides	Third party provides	Developer provides
Tasks in setting up Change Management					
consider who to involve in the Change Advisory Board		✓		✓	
define special arrangements for urgent changes		✓	✓	✓	
Tasks in Change Management					
processing RFCs		✓	✓		✓
change scheduling	✓				
change building				✓	✓
change recording		✓		✓	✓
implementation		✓		✓	✓

A.3.5 Configuration Management

	ITSM provides	ITSM jointly provides	Business provides	Third party provides	Developer provides
Tasks in configuration identification					
deciding the scope of items to be controlled		✓		✓	
deciding the level of items to be controlled, keeping a balance between the availability of information and the resources you'll need to collect and maintain it		✓		✓	
defining a naming convention		✓		✓	
recording all Configuration Items (CIs), their attributes and the relationships between them in a Configuration Management Database (CMDB)		✓		✓	
Status accounting (recording and reporting the current and historical status of each CI)					
recording all changes to CIs in the CMDB	✓				
producing periodic status reports listing current CIs and their status	✓				
Verification (reviewing or auditing process which makes sure that all CIs conform with their records in the CMDB)					
checking physical CIs against status reports, confirming location, owner, specification etc.		✓	✓	✓	

A.3.6 Release Management

	ITSM provides	ITSM jointly provides	Business provides	Third party provides	Developer provides
authorising releases	✓				
defining releases	✓				✓
controlling releases	✓				
maintaining the Definitive Software Library (DSL)	✓			✓	✓
bringing software into service		✓	✓		✓
Tasks in setting up Release Management					
all new or changed services to be rigorously tested, where possible, before live running				✓	✓
all releases to be tested for compatibility with the rest of the organisation's IT infrastructure	✓			✓	

A.3.7 Service Level Management

	ITSM provides	ITSM jointly provides	Business provides	Third party provides	Developer provides
creating a service catalogue		✓	✓	✓	
identifying service level requirements		✓	✓		✓
negotiating Service Level Agreements (SLAs)	✓				
reviewing support services				✓	
setting accounting policies		✓	✓	✓	
monitoring and reviewing services	✓		✓	✓	
reporting	✓				

A.3.8 Finance Management

	ITSM provides	ITSM jointly provides	Business provides	Third party provides	Developer provides
General tasks					
establishing accounting – knowing what the costs of providing IT services are		✓	✓	✓	
optionally, implementing charging – recovering costs from users		✓		✓	
Detailed tasks – planning annually					
accounting – establishing the standard unit costs for each major IT service		✓		✓	
charging – establishing a pricing portfolio and a 'price list' for each item		✓		✓	
preparing and agreeing budgets for ITSM		✓			
Operations (perhaps monthly)					
monitoring expenditure and comparing plans to actuals by cost unit	✓				
compiling and issuing invoices		✓		✓	

A.3.9   Capacity Management

	ITSM provides	ITSM jointly provides	Business provides	Third party provides	Developer provides
maintaining the Capacity Management data		✓		✓	
producing reports		✓		✓	
producing capacity plans				✓	
monitoring performance		✓		✓	
managing resources	✓			✓	✓
managing demand		✓	✓		
Tasks in structuring the Capacity Management function					
deciding if mainframe, midrange, PC and network capacity can be managed together by the same person or group		✓		✓	
deciding if the capacity planning and performance monitoring elements should be split		✓		✓	

A.3.10 Availability Management

	ITSM provides	ITSM jointly provides	Business provides	Third party provides	Developer provides
Managing reliability					
measuring the reliability of each part of the infrastructure	✓				
specifying the resilience built into the IT service		✓		✓	✓
agreeing the level of preventative maintenance		✓		✓	
Managing service availability					
keeping IT in operation (maintainability)	✓			✓	✓
managing serviceability	✓			✓	
Tasks in the availability planning process					
determining what availability requirements are	✓		✓		
designing for availability		✓		✓	
producing the availability plan		✓		✓	
Tasks in the monitoring and reporting of availability					
collecting availability data	✓				
maintaining the availability database		✓		✓	
monitoring how IT services comply to availability requirements in SLAs and how contractors comply to serviceability requirements	✓				
reporting achieved availability levels to the service level manager and other IT service managers	✓				

A.3.11 IT Service Continuity Management

	ITSM provides	ITSM jointly provides	Business provides	Third party provides	Developer provides
understanding what options for disaster recovery are available and choosing the right one		✓	✓	✓	
Tasks in the ITSCM process					
analysing the impact of a disaster on the business and what countermeasures are justified (using CRAMM (CCTA Risk Assessment and Management Method))				✓	
producing the contingency plan		✓	✓	✓	
regularly testing and reviewing the contingency plan		✓	✓	✓	

Annex B SUGGESTED CONTENTS FOR A USER HANDBOOK

B.1 Introduction

What a user handbook contains will, like everything else mentioned in this book, depend on the organisation being considered. There may even be a need to produce different versions within a single organisation if there is a clearly differentiated customer base. The following suggested potential contents are offered as a guide and a possible starting point for building an organisation's own user handbook.

B.2 Universal items

There are some elements that one would expect to find in every organisation's user handbook. While there may well be exceptions in unusual circumstances, it would be hard to see why an organisation would not wish to ensure their customers and users were aware of the following:

- what services the IT organisation supports
- help and advice
- glossary of terms
- procedures relating to changes
- security issues.

B.2.1 What services the IT organisation supports

A catalogue of the services available to users, how to access them, and what they provide in terms of business support.

B.2.2 Help and advice

This part of the handbook would cover:

- simple things that can (and should) be checked before turning elsewhere for help
- where and how to get help from, for example:
  - local systems administrators
  - Service Desk

- how to report issues and faults, when services are available, the information to gather together first, priority allocation practices, what the categories mean, what rights the users have in categorising, rights of appeal in case of disagreement.

B.2.3   Glossary of terms

While jargon should be avoided wherever possible, its use is inevitable. In a handbook designed to be referred to many times, its total avoidance will make explanations overlong, the book difficult to refer to quickly when required and tedious to read on subsequent occasions. All jargon that is used must be defined in simple terms. One useful option can be to define the word near the text where it is used, as well as in a separate glossary.

The handbook is not an IT document; it is intended to support business users and will thus also contain jargon appropriate to whatever business is being supported. This jargon needs to be defined along with any IT jargon used. Concise and easy to understand definitions will aid new users, often those most in need of the IT handbook, who are likely to be unfamiliar with the business terms, as well as the IT ones. The most difficult jargon of all to cope with is the specialised usage of what, elsewhere, would be a word of general meaning. A very common example is the use made of the word 'quality'.

B.2.4   Procedures relating to changes

This section would include:

- change requests – the format required, where to submit them, what does and what doesn't require formal requests for change and prior approval, time scales for approval or rejection and any appeals procedures
- urgent change procedures – especially authority to define a change as urgent and rules on what might constitute 'urgent'
- notification of changes to ITSM – how users will be informed of staff changes and moves, new phone numbers, contact points etc., minor moves of equipment (where permitted).

B.2.5   Security issues

This has two areas of coverage:

- protection of data, for example:
  - control of passwords
  - measures in place to protect against viruses and hacking
  - procedures for backing up data and programs and for recovering back-up software

- legal aspects, such as:
  - – Data Protection Act implications, especially on local software applications
  - – software licensing and copyright.

B.3 Probable items for inclusion

Elements that would typically appear, and are certainly worth considering for inclusion in most organisations, include the following:

- procurement of IT equipment
- basics of using the service
- auditing.

B.3.1 Procurement of IT equipment

Where users have the authority to purchase IT equipment for use within their business areas, the handbook would be likely to contain sections on:

- Purchasing hardware and software products which are recommended and/or supported by the IT organisation. Products might include typical PC configurations and software packages suitable for different types of users and applications
- Advice on selecting and buying which might range from a simple recommendation to use the IT organisation for purchasing, to guidance on comparison and evaluating value for money over the whole lifetime of a product.

B.3.2 Basics of using the service

This section would reflect the customers and users which the IT organisation supports. Its main purpose is to try and establish a baseline level of knowledge which the Service Desk can assume is possessed by callers.

B.3.3 Auditing

This section covers the need for cooperation in audits of hardware and software carried out by ITSM. This might include:

- ITSM's rights of access to data (could be a significant issue requiring negotiation and documented accessing if restricted data is being processed)
- the need to label all items
- the use of personal software on the organisation's IT equipment.

B.4   Possible items for inclusion

Depending on the organisation, anything of relevance should be included. As the handbook becomes more used and an automatic first place to look for help, other sections may wish to have material included, from fire alarm procedures to welfare services and cafeteria facilities. Balance the benefits against the drawbacks.

Benefits of combining with other sections include:

- wide coverage and content mean wide interest in keeping it up to date
- single source of reference is more likely to be kept handy and actually referred to
- economies of scale in production
- likelihood of spotting overlaps and/or inconsistencies between procedures established by different sections.

Drawbacks of combining with other sections include:

- handbook becomes too large and cumbersome to use
- too much content, allied to bad or non-existent indexing, means you can't find the bit you want
- inevitable inconsistencies appear
- ownership becomes shared resulting in intractable committees deciding on format, reviews and content. This:
    - delays updates, making it more likely to be out of date
    - prevents innovative use of presentational techniques
    - is likely to result in a stodgy prose style, after everyone has added their comments to proposed content.

B.5   Ownership and maintenance

It must be clear who is responsible for keeping the guide up to date. A policy on encouraging suggestions and updates needs to be put in place and followed. While for an IT-only handbook, full ownership would be with ITSM, if the IT guidance forms part of a larger document, or more typically nowadays, an intranet service, ownership of the whole product, covering update periods and methods, access rights etc. may rest elsewhere. Nonetheless ownership of the IT service user guidance should remain with a designated person within ITSM. Management of crucial 'shred' components, such as the glossary of terms, needs careful administration to ensure they deliver the required support to all areas using them.

INDEX

References to figures are shown in **bold**.